The Professional Programmers Guide to
**UNIX**

GW01425156

The Professional Programmers Guide to

# UNIX

**Richard J Bird**
Newcastle upon Tyne Polytechnic

Pitman

PITMAN PUBLISHING
128 Long Acre London WC2E 9AN

© Richard J Bird 1988

First published in Great Britain 1988

**British Library Cataloguing in Publication Data**

Bird, Richard, *1938–*
    The professional programmer's guide to
    UNIX.—(Professional programmers guides).
    1. UNIX (Computer operating system)
    I. Title
    005.4'3        QA76.76.063

    ISBN 0–273–02855–3

Printed and bound in Great Britain at
The Bath Press, Avon

UNIX is a registered trademark of AT&T Bell Laboratories.

# Contents

**Introduction**   vii

**1   Structured Operating Systems   1**
1.1 The origins of operating systems   1
1.2 The functions of an operating system   2
1.3 Operating system organisation   4
1.4 File handling in UNIX   6
1.5 UNIX command style   8

**2   UNIX Fundamentals   11**
2.1 Logging on to UNIX   11
2.2 Making a file – the text editor   12
2.3 Using directories   15
2.4 A survey of file handling commands   20
2.5 Some simple commands   22

**3   The UNIX File System   36**
3.1 File structure   36
3.2 The file system   37
3.3 File types   37
3.4 Redirection   43
3.5 File security   44
3.6 File handling commands   46
3.7 Mapping the file system   50

**4   Pipes and Forks   58**
4.1 The shell   58
4.2 Pipes   61
4.3 Shell scripts   64
4.4 Filters   64
4.5 Flow control   67
4.6 Substitutable parameters   69
4.7 String variables   71
4.8 The environment   72
4.9 Executable files   74
4.10 Alternative shells   74

## 5 The C Programming Language 76

5.1 The importance of C to UNIX 76
5.2 Characteristics of C 77
5.3 Structure of a C program 78
5.4 Writing C programs 79
5.5 Programming style 83
5.6 Arithmetic in C 84
5.7 Input and output 85
5.8 More on typing 86
5.9 Block structure 88
5.10 Functions 90

## 6 Text Handling in UNIX 96

6.1 The text editor – ed 96
6.2 The screen editor 108
6.3 Text formatting 113
6.4 File processing commands 117
6.5 Pattern recognition and processing – awk 118
6.6 The stream editor – sed 119
6.7 Lexical analysis program generator – lex 120
6.8 Input structuring program – yacc 122

## 7 Use and Superuse 125

7.1 The need for a superuser 125
7.2 Signing on as superuser 126
7.3 Adding new users 126
7.4 Removing users 131
7.5 System startup 132
7.6 System checks 133
7.7 Mounting and unmounting file systems 136
7.8 Bringing the system down 136

## 8 The Varieties of UNIX 138

8.1 Many types of UNIX 138
8.2 Bell Labs UNIXes 142
8.3 AT&T licensed versions 144
8.4 UNIX-like systems 146

## Index 149

# Introduction

This book is an introduction to the UNIX operating system for the computer-literate reader who wishes to acquire UNIX skills. Familiarity with some hardware and software is assumed, but these need not be of any specific variety.

The text is an attempt not simply to list commands and facilities and how to use them but also to give an insight into the way that UNIX works. With this understanding readers should be able to work out a lot of things for themselves which might otherwise be obscure.

All the interactive examples in the text are actual interactions with UNIX. The reader can therefore sit at a terminal with these parts of the text and follow the examples on a character-for-character basis.

The text goes from the level of the first elements of use of the system through to the role of the system supervisor. The book ends with a brief review of current implementations of UNIX in the marketplace.

UNIX users are typically one of two genders, but as the English language does not yet offer any androgynous pronouns, those I have used throughout the book should be interpreted as meaning both.

R. J. Bird
January 1988

# 1 Structured Operating Systems

## 1.1 The Origins of Operating Systems

In the early days of computing there were no operating systems. The user was faced with a computer which, when switched on, was a 'tabula rasa' – a blank piece of paper, waiting to be written on. To get the computer to perform any useful function the programmer first had to get a program into the machine. Since the computer contained no program he was faced with a circular problem; how to get a computer with no program inside it to read in a program.

The problem was solved by means of something called a 'bootstrap'. This was itself a program, either permanently built into the computer's memory or loaded in from a switch register. The bootstrap consisted of a few instructions to read in further instructions, thus reading in whole programs 'by their bootstraps'.

The next difficulty which the user faced was how to get the required information into his program and how to get the results out. In the early days, input devices were usually either paper tape or punched card readers. In order to read the required data, the user had to ensure that the cards (say) were loaded into the reader, that when they ran out the program knew about it, and that more cards were then loaded if necessary. When the end of the card deck was reached ('end of file') the program also had to detect this condition and begin processing the data it had ingested. When the program was finished (or while it was still running) the results had to be output, usually either by printing them on a Teletype or by punching them on to paper tape; so the user program had to carry out the necessary output operations too, when required.

At the end of a program the computer had to be cleared of that job and readied to begin execution of the next one. This involved several steps. It meant ensuring that the input and output devices were freed of the material used by the first program. Cards had to be taken out of the reader and the punch, and paper tape removed from the paper tape station. The memory had to be cleared and/or over-written by the image of the new program. This usually involved a manual operation at the console, followed by the re-use of the bootstrap to load the next job. All these functions had to be carried out between jobs by the operator, and they slowed the transition between one job and the next considerably.

Another aspect of computing in the early days was the fact that only one person could use the machine at any one time. Whatever the user was doing, whether it was running a program, assembling it or debugging it, the system was dedicated to that one user. The result was that what was in those days an expensive device was fully occupied while a programmer just sat and thought in front of the console.

Without operating systems to assist them, programmers and operators were unable to make full use of their machines. From the programmer's point of view, a lot of time had to be spent repeating the same work of programming input and output of data, testing for end of file conditions and so on. Nor was it easy for the programmer to gain access to what are now called utilities – the software which helps in the development work and at run-time. To call one program from within another was hard enough, but to return to the first program again or to alternate freely between program images was virtually impossible.

From the point of view of the operator of such a system, things were little better. A lot of manual intervention was called for. Each time a job was run, the newly readied computer had to be reloaded via a bootstrap procedure. Additionally, devices had to be serviced frequently, with special attention to conditions arising at the end of a job. It was in response to such difficulties that the first operating systems were developed.

## 1.2   The Functions of an Operating System

This look back into the distant past gives some clue to the functions of a modern operating system. Such a system will look after most of the aspects of job scheduling, file handling and device control, leaving the programmer free to work on his problem and enabling the operator to concentrate his attention on more important aspects of the functioning of the computer.

To begin with, there is no longer any need to worry about 'bootstrap programs'. These survive merely in the expression 'booting the system' – at worst only a matter of pressing one or two keys on the console at the start of the day. Because part of the operating system (the 'monitor') is permanently resident in memory, jobs are loaded into memory when the appropriate command is given. A series of jobs can be run from a command file, which contains the necessary instructions and which can itself be executed as a job. Statistical data about jobs can also be accumulated, and the output tagged with date and time of execution. Using such facilities automatic logging of computer usage is now commonplace.

The next difficulty faced by the pioneer programmers, the input and output of data, has been greatly reduced by the way in which modern operating systems handle devices and the information which they process. The contemporary 'device handler' looks after the problems of physical maintenance and allows the user to address all his devices in more or less the same way. For example, you can tell a program to list a file on the listing device (which may be a printer or a typewriter), to punch it on to paper tape or to write it to a file (on floppy or hard disk), without changing anything but the device names. The device handlers in the operating system will do the necessary housekeeping, such as checking for disk errors, punching run-out tape and feeding paper when required. The writer of the software need not concern himself much with the detailed operation of these devices: all he needs to do is call the appropriate device handler, and pass a few parameters to it.

Furthermore, the information to be sent to each of these kinds of device can be handled in much the same way. There is no need to worry about device-specific details such as tabulation stops, blanks or device-specific write operations; these are allowed for when necessary by the device handler. This means that information can be structured according to its own logic rather than according to the requirements of the device on which it is output. (Not all operating systems are quite as sophisticated as this, as we shall see, but the better ones are.) Another way of saying the same thing is that operating systems nowadays look after file handling as well as device handling. How they handle files is a matter to which we shall return later.

The availablity of utility programs is no longer a problem either. If an operating system is based on disk there is a minimal swapping time involved in getting a program loaded into memory. This means, for example, that an editor can be rapidly invoked to allow the re-compilation of a corrected program text, or that a debugging aid can be installed with the minimum amount of trouble.

So we can see that operating systems help in at least four separate ways: by looking after job control, by providing device handling facilities, by handling data in files and by making the provision of utility software easier. What sort of methods do operating systems use to achieve these results?

## 1.3 Operating System Organisation

First of all, no serious operating system can work with anything below a disk. There are good cheap ROM-based operating systems for small machines, but they offer very limited facilities. In any case, no sophisticated system is available which is not based at least on floppy disks. Tape-based operating systems are feasible, but are intolerably slow for most purposes.

Given that a user has disk space available to him on the system, it is natural that he will keep his program and data files there. Disks are by their nature file-oriented devices; by contrast with, say, printers and keyboards, which are not. (A file-oriented device means one which allows for the handling of more than one nameable file at a time. You can save and load files on disk at will, and they will remain known to the system by name, unless this is deliberately changed.)

## File Organisation

If you have disk space available for storing files, it is sensible to adopt some sort of system for file organisation. There is a certain amount of information which you need to know in order to be able to store and retrieve a file easily: for example its length and what kind of file it is. There are other pieces of information which are desirable also, such as when the file was created (this is useful if more than one version of the same file is in existence at the same time.) To be able to save files on disk and get them back again, this information must itself be stored somewhere on the disk, in readily accessible form.

### Directories

This sort of reasoning led to the introduction of directories. A directory is an area of the file-storage device which holds the information about files which is necessary for their storage, maintenance and retrieval. The directory will tell you the name of a file, its type (possibly as part of the name) and its length, and may hold other information about it too. The directory also knows how much storage space on the device has been used, and how much is left free to use. The directory is absolutely indispensible to the organisation of any file-system. The organisation of the directory is therefore of crucial importance also.

The first thought about the organisation of a directory was that it should be a simple list of entries. (In other words, the directory was *unstructured*.) It was of course true that the system as a whole could contain a number of directories; one (or even more) for each user. But the directories themselves retained the same structure, or lack of structure, lending an inherent lack of structure to the whole system. Some operating systems still keep this way of organising directories and hence the file structure associated with them: others do not.

## *File types*

The next question of importance to the designer of an operating system is how to handle different kinds of file. There are many ways of organising data into files. You can write it as a series of binary numbers (think of it as being written to disk in the form of words, with a convention for deciding what the words mean later) or as a series of 'records', each record corresponding to an individual case, or as 'lines' of text. Files used for different purposes will require different structures: for instance, a file which contains a program ready for execution will have a different structure from a data file consisting of a series of numeric or alphanumeric values. Each different kind of file will need to be treated in a different way when it is used.

Is it possible to have an operating system which can handle so many different types of file conveniently? (Different operating systems have solved this problem in different ways: all of the solutions are compromises but some are better than others.)

## Device handling

A linked problem is how to treat the different types of device in the system. If the operating system is designed for only one possible device configuration then the problem is not so great. But operating systems today have to be able to cope with any of the commonly used kinds of device which may be attached (e.g. terminals of different kinds, or different types of disk storage device). In order to deal satisfactorily with all these possibilities, there has to be a library of device handlers which can supply the one needed whenever the operating system is set up in a particular hardware environment. This process (known as configuring the system) is now an important part of the facilities offered by operating system software.

## Job control

As we have seen, operating systems are designed to make the transition between one job and another easier. The ways in which they can do this are manifold. The most basic is the control which is available through the use of the operating system command language. By giving commands to the operating system itself, the user can attach devices to the system, copy files from one device to another, assemble programs and run them, and do many other things.

It is clear that if the commands to do these things can be stored in a file, they can be carried out indirectly by giving a command to the system to obey the commands in that file. In this way, the commands necessary to set up and run a series of jobs can be stored in another special type of file – the command file. Nearly all operating systems offer this kind of facility, which to some extent detaches the job inputs and outputs from the limited context of the job itself, and which also enhances the power of the command language.

## Command language

The command language itself is at the heart of the facilities offered by any operating system. Whether you can do a lot of things or only a few, how much you can do with a single command and how the commands link together with one another, these are the simplest measures of the power of the system. For example, in RT-11, which is a prototypical operating system of one particular kind, you can support more than one console device, but not at the same time. RT-11 is therefore not an operating system for a multi-user environment although it offers good facilities to a single user. UNIX, on the other hand, is inherently an operating system which lends itself to multi-user applications. In UNIX you can have multi-user access to the system's facilities without much mutual awareness of one another's presence. You also get the use of some very powerful system calls which give each user a flexible multiprogramming environment. Let us now see how UNIX achieves this, and how it solves the other problems which have been outlined.

## 1.4   File Handling in UNIX

It is probably a good idea to start at a central point by looking at the way in which UNIX deals with files. This has two aspects: the way in which files are handled, and the way in which a file is structured internally. Files in UNIX resemble those in other systems: they are primarily collections of data stored on some device (usually a disk) for easy access. However the concept of 'file' is extended in UNIX to embrace any stream of input or output; for example the data coming from a terminal keyboard, or the information being output to a line printer. This means that all such streams of data can be treated in the same way, not only as far as the syntax of commands is concerned but also from the point of view of the system.

This equivalence of different file types from the system's viewpoint is assisted by the structure of the files themselves. Only one type of file is allowed in canonical UNIX – a string of bytes. No special provision is made for blocking, records or other subdivision of the file at the level of the file-handlers. This has the effect of simplifying the writing of the file-handling part of the system enormously, since no special measures need to be taken to count blocks, check record lengths, etc. This attitude to file structure solves many problems and raises some as well. Users sometimes feel at a loss to know how to structure their files, simply because the system does not do it for them. However, the structure imposed by some systems is quite arbitrary. (Eighty-character records, for example, are simply a survival from the days of punched cards.) Structure is still available just as before, only now it is at the level of the user's system and not the operating system. Everyone does not need to accept the same system-imposed structure!

The concept of file is extended in UNIX to another important area – that of device handling. Devices are treated by the system in the same way as files; in fact, they are files so far as getting and putting information is concerned. This allows a very flexible approach to devices, because it lets the user transpose files and devices, and frees him of the worry of how to address them. He need not concern himself with the type of device he is using – at least as far as the handler is concerned – in fact he need not even know whether he is using a device or not! (This attitude to files and devices has far-reaching consequences, as we shall see.)

Files which are used for storage are accessed through a directory in the same way as in other operating systems. But in UNIX there is a big difference: there is not just one directory for each user, but as many as are needed. Furthermore, a directory can be treated just like a file. A directory can be entered in another directory, and so on, in a series of descending 'nodes'. In this way a user can build up a structure of directories, each containing files and/or pointers to other directories.

In some of the early UNIX systems the way in which the structure grew was quite free: so that for example a directory could be an entry in any other directory, making the structure a freely-directed graph of a general kind. It was soon found that this gave rise to serious problems. (For example, a series of directories could be interconnected in this way but all the other files might have been deleted. The system would then have no way of knowing that the directories themselves were no longer needed.) At present, UNIX allows only a 'tree' directory structure to be grown, with each directory-node having a 'parent', and, possibly, children of its own. In this way the complications of cross-referencing between directories (and possibly between devices which hold the directories) can be largely avoided.

## 1.5 UNIX Command Style

The second major innovative feature of UNIX is the way in which the commands are designed to interact freely with one another and with their environment. This gives rise to a feature of UNIX which is quite noticeable to the new user – its rather terse style. There are not a lot of elaborate diagnostics written into the system, and this is for a good reason: UNIX commands are designed to be easily interfaced with one another, by means of the mechanism of 'pipes'.

A pipe is a link between the output of one command and the input of another, so that processing can be continuous. The commands are therefore written in such a way that they expect input in a processable form, without unnecessary preambles or extraneous messages surrounding it.

For example the word count command *wc* inspects the contents of a file and counts the number of lines, words or characters in it. Since the file it accepts may be the output from another command, it would obviously be inaccurate in its count if the input were cluttered with diagnostic messages such as 'EXECUTION BEGINS', 'EXECUTION TERMINATED' etc. Commands are designed in UNIX to operate 'silently'; that is, if all goes well there is no message. If something goes wrong, the message is likely to be terse, perhaps just a '?'. On the other hand, UNIX is often quite helpful when giving advice about how to use its facilities. Commands which are incorrectly used often reply with comments about their usage, and there is a good deal of on-line help about the facilities of the system.

Sometimes this terseness is interpreted by users as 'unfriendliness' on the part of the system. At the moment there is a lot of emphasis on the idea of user-friendliness, and rightly so. But the question is, who is a better friend: one who keeps interrupting you when you want to explain yourself, or one who follows you silently because he understands you?

As well as being able to interact with one another, commands in UNIX are free to direct their output and input to any file or device. The symbol '<' used in a command means 'take your input from' and '>' means 'send your input to', and these symbols can be followed by file or device names. For example, the command:

```
$ cat filea fileb filec >filed
```

will concatenate the three files 'filea', 'fileb' and 'filec' and put the new file in 'filed'. Similarly the command:

```
$ crypt <cypher
```

will take its input from the file 'cypher', decrypt it and output it to the terminal.

An extension of the flexible use of command input and output is the ability to write programs in the UNIX command language. For instance, suppose the following commands are put into a file:

```
mkdir newdir
chmod go -r newdir
cd newdir
```

If the file name is now given as a command, a new directory called 'newdir' will be created in the working directory, permission to read it will be denied to other users, and then the new directory will become the working directory.

The creation and execution of a program written in the command language of UNIX in this way is extremely useful. It is done by means of the UNIX command decoder, which is known as the 'shell'. The shell is a program which interprets commands and commences their execution. It is running all the time from when the user logs in, ready to carry out this function, and when a command has been executed, control is returned to the shell ready for the next incoming command from the terminal.

The shell is able, by a device which will be described more fully in Chapter 4, to execute not only single commands but also files containing lists of commands. It does this by creating a parallel execution environment for commands, known as a 'process', in which the commands are carried out. When the commands have been executed the process is terminated and control once more returns to the shell. As we will see in Chapter 4, the ability to write shell programs is a powerful feature of UNIX.

From this brief account it can be seen that UNIX and UNIX-like operating systems offer many useful features. File handling, device control and job control are all straightforward. To fully appreciate the virtues of UNIX however it is necessary to learn to use it: the next chapter is a tutorial introduction to the system and to some of the commands and facilities available within it.

# 2 UNIX Fundamentals

## 2.1 Logging on to UNIX

The first thing you must do when confronted by a terminal running the UNIX system is to log in. The terminal will be displaying the message

```
login:
```

In reply to this you must type your user name and press return to enter the line into the computer. The system will then respond with

```
password:
```

in reponse to which you enter your password (which will not, however, be echoed by the terminal, in the interests of security). The whole dialogue looks like this:

```
login: name
password: <password>
```

(N.B. To distinguish what the user types from what the system outputs, throughout this text the user's input will be shown in bold type.)

The system will respond by printing the message-of-the-day and informing you of any mail which may be waiting for you. The system then awaits further input after printing out a prompt character, usually '$'. You are now logged on to UNIX.

## Logging off

Conventions for logging off vary. In some systems the command:

```
$ logout
```

is used. In other systems it is sufficient to type ^D (Control-D) or occasionally ^C.

## The home directory

When you have logged in, you are in a directory which has had a name given to it by the system: it will probably be your own name. If my directory is called *richard* I will be in this directory whenever I sign on. This directory is called the user's home directory.

Once you are in your home directory you have access to the files in it by simply specifying their names (files in other directories can only be accessed by giving their directory name first.) If you have just signed on for the first time you probably have no files, in which case it is a useful exercise to create one or two.

## 2.2 Making a File – the Text Editor

To make a file you can use the standard text editor *ed* which you run with the command

```
$ ed [filename]
```

If you give a file name to *ed* it will assume a file with that name already exists and will look for it. If it doesn't find a file of that name in the current directory, *ed* assumes that you want one created, and it will remember the name for use as a default in the next write command.

If you omit the name (as the square brackets indicate you may) you can begin entering lines into a text buffer and write them out later naming the file at that stage. Suppose you do the following:

```
$ ed file1
```

You are now in the editor, which is waiting for commands. (These commands are on a different level from the other UNIX commands. Editor commands allow you, among other things, to input text, to search for and alter strings and to list the contents of the file you are editing.)

## Adding text

Now you can put something into the newly created file, *file1*. To insert text, use the editor append command *a* like this;

```
a
<text>
.
```

The *a* command goes on a line by itself. The editor then accepts the text which follows, including return and other special characters, until it reads a single period on a line by itself. The editor then ceases to read text and you are back in editor command mode.

The lines are stored in an area called the text buffer, and they are given numbers from 1 onwards, by which you can refer to them (as we shall soon see.)

Suppose the following command has been carried out:

```
a
This is the first line
This is the second line
This is line three
This is the fourth line
This is the last line
```

## Listing the text buffer

The buffer now contains five lines. You can list these using the editor list command *l*. This allows you to specify the numbers of the lines you want listed. To list the contents of the entire text buffer you type:

```
1,$l
This is the first line
This is the second line
This is line three
This is the fourth line
This is the last line
```

### *Line numbers*

The string '1,$' means 'list from line 1 to the last line' (by convention, the last line in the buffer is referred to by the character $.) The more general form of the *l* command is thus:

```
(.,.)l
```

where '.' represents any line number.

## Substituting text

If you make mistakes while putting material into a file, you can correct them while you are still in *ed*. In the above example we have named line three inconsistently. To correct this you can use the search and replace command *s* as follows:

```
1,$s/line three/the third line/
```

This command searches the text buffer between lines 1 and $ for the string between the first and second '/' characters and replaces it with the string between the second and third '/' characters. If you now list the contents of the file, it will look like this:

```
1,$1
This is the first line
This is the second line
This is the third line
This is the fourth line
This is the last line
```

## Writing to a file

You can now write the contents of the buffer to the file previously created, using *w* :

```
w
116
```

The number '116' is a count of the number of bytes written from the buffer.

## Leaving the text editor

It would now be possible to continue to use the editor to create or alter other files, or even to make further alterations to file1. But if you don't want to do any more editing, you can exit from *ed* by the quit command:

```
q
```

The file you have created is now in your home directory. You can see that it is there by using the command *ls* which lists the contents of a directory:

```
$ ls
file1
```

## The screen editor

A version of the editor which may be preferred by the beginner is the

14

version of *ed* called *em* or 'editor for mortals'. This version has certain features which make the editor easier to use.

For example, *em* keeps a log of the editing session so that in the event of a system crash, your work will be recoverable. Giving the command:

```
$ em -r <logfile>
```

the editor will re-create the editing session for you. *em* also offers various other features which may assist the user (see Chapter 6).

The line editors *ed* are the ones most frequently used by UNIX professionals. There are alternatives to using the line editor, which may be simpler for the beginner or the non-programmer. One of these is the screen editor *vi*. You can invoke this by means of the command:

```
$ vi <filename>
```

You will then see a screen which looks like this:

```
~
~
~
~
~
~
~
~
~
.
.
.
'filename' [new file]
```

if 'filename' is a new file. If it is an existing file, you will see the first few lines of the file printed out on the screen instead of the tildes. You can then edit the file from the keyboard and see the changes take place in front of you on the screen. Further details of *vi* are given in Chapter 6.

## 2.3  Using Directories

### Listing files

When you are not using the editor you can still list the contents of files on your terminal by using the command *cat*. *cat* is a command which concatenates one or more files together and directs them to a destination. If you do not specify the destination, the new file will be written to the standard output, which is your terminal. If only one file is specified then effectively *cat* lists that file. Thus:

```
$ cat file1
This is the first line
This is the second line
This is the third line
This is the fourth line
This is the last line
```

lists your file for you.

Some people find it confusing at first that there is no easily identifiable 'list' command for printing out files, and attempts have been made to get *cat* changed to another name. But using *cat* for both concatenation and listing saves having two commands where one will do. Besides, its use in this way is just a convention, and is soon got used to.

You can also list a file using the command *pr*, which will print it out on the terminal in a paginated (page formatted) form. In a file like the present one, which is very short, it is probably not worth paginating the output.

When you log in you are in the home directory: the directory which was created for you by the person in charge of the system (the super-user.) So far you have remained within that directory. But it is both easy and convenient to create other directories for your use: perhaps to keep together files which are in a particular category. The tree-like structure of UNIX directories allows you to make categories which are subordinate to one another as required.

## Making directories

The command *mkdir* will create a new directory, making it an entry in your current directory, e.g.

```
$ mkdir john
```

If your home directory is called *richard* then *john* will now become an entry in *richard*.

## Listing directories

You are still in your home directory. If you now list the directory you will see two entries:

```
$ ls
```

```
john
file1
```

There are one or two points of interest about this simple listing of a directory. First, directory entries may be either files or may themselves be directories. In the kind of listing shown above it is not clear which they are. There are different forms of the *ls* command which allow you to see what kinds of entry a directory contains. We shall have a look at some of these in a moment.

It is also worth noticing that the order of the listed entries is not necessarily the same as the order in which they were created: they have been sorted into alphabetic sequence. We can alter the way in which directories are listed by modifying the *ls* command.

For example, it is possible to list them by the order of their creation, rather than alphabetically, from the most recent to the least recent, using:

```
$ ls -t
file1
john
```

The string '-t' is known as a flag, and modifies the *ls* command accordingly. Most commands in UNIX employ flags to give the user options about how to use the commands. The more general form of a command is thus:

```
command [flags] [name]
```

where the strings in square brackets may be omitted as appropriate. (Square brackets will be used to indicate optional parts of the input throughout.)

Some commands do not require a filename or other name (operand) to operate on. The operand may be implicit, or, as in the case of the *ed* command, a command may invoke a process with no specified input. Flags are always optional.

In the case of the *ls* command, the flag -t modifies the command to sort its output by time of creation rather than by name, which would be the default function of the command.

If we use the flag '-l' we get the following listing:

```
$ ls -l
total 4
drwx------  3 richard         96 Apr 13 20:27 john
-rwxrwxrwx  1 richard        116 Mar  9 20:01 file1
```

For each file in the directory listed there is a set of characters, which have the following meanings:

The first character is 'd' if the file is a directory, '-' if it is an ordinary file. The next nine characters are the permission bits which allow the file to be read, written to, or, if a program, executed. These permissions apply to three groups of users and can be set by means of the *chmod* command (see page 40).

The number of links to the file is then given (see page 38) the owner's name, the number of bytes in the file, the date of its creation and the time, and finally the filename.

## Pathnames

You have now created a directory *john* which is an entry in *richard*, your home directory, but you are still in *richard*. If you want to refer to a file in *john* you can do so by using its *pathname*, that is, the route by which the file can be located from some specified starting place. If you are starting from *richard,* the pathname of a file in *john* would be:

```
john/file
```

A pathname follows certain conventions: in this case the slashes '/' are used to separate directories at successive levels of the tree leading to the file. You could, for instance, list the contents of a file named *file* in directory *john* by:

```
$ cat john/file
```

(although since there is no file in *john* at the moment, you would not get a listing.)

## Copying files

Let us remedy this lack of a file in *john*. We can do this in a number of ways: one is to copy an existing file, say *file1*, into the new directory, using the copy command *cp* thus:

```
$ cp file1 john/file2
```

We can now list the new file by specifying its pathname from the current working directory (which is also the home directory):

```
$ cat john/file2
This is the first line
This is the second line
This is the third line
This is the fourth line
This is the last line
```

## Changing directories

Another way of gaining access to *file2* in *john* is by changing directories from your home directory *richard* to *john*. This is done by means of the change directory command *cd*. Thus:

```
$ cd john
```

puts you into *john* as the working directory. Once in *john*, its files can be directly addressed, and you can list *file2* by saying:

```
$ cat file2
This is the first line
This is the second line
This is the third line
This is the fourth line
This is the last line
```

The contents of *file2* and those of *file1* are unfortunately identical (since one is a copy of the other.) When we list the two files we get the same output. Let's change the contents of one of them, say *file2*, by using *ed* as follows:

```
$ ed file2
116
1,$s/last line/last line./
1,$l
This is the first line
This is the second line
This is the third line
This is the fourth line
This is the last line.
w
117
q
```

Spot the difference between file2 and file1. There is now a period at the end of the last line of file2. This may seem trivial, but it can be used to illustrate the power of some UNIX commands quite well.

## Printing current directory

Remember we are now in directory *john*. If you forget which directory you are in, you can find out by giving the command

```
$ pwd
/user/richard/john
```

This tells you not only that you are in *john* but also how to get there.

The starting point in this case is the directory '/', which is known as the *root* of the file system. Within the root directory there are a number of other files and directories, and one of these is a directory called *user*. *user* holds the home directories of all the users on the system. Your home directory is (we have assumed) *richard*. You have created a directory within your home directory, and this now forms a new level of the downward-branching tree. The complete path name is therefore that shown in reply to the *pwd* command above.

Now you are in directory *john* you can directly address all files in it – that is, you need only give the filename and not the pathname from any other directory. In order to address a file in another directory, you must specify the pathname in the appropriate way.

The rules for giving pathnames are fairly commonsense. If you are in *richard* you can get a file in *john* by specifying the pathname *john*. But if you are in *john,* to get a file in *richard* you must give the pathname */user/richard*. You cannot get it by using the pathname *richard* alone.

The sequence of directories and filenames which must be specified to arrive at the target depends on the starting point. A quick way of changing directory is sometimes to use the dot construction.

### Parent and child directories

The command:

    $ cd ..

will change the working directory to the next furthest from the root directory. Thus, we could change from *john* to *richard* by this command. The directory *richard* is said to be the parent of the directory *john*.

Similarly we could change from *john* to another directory in *richard* ( *jack* say) by the command:

    $ cd ../jack

This effectively changes you up one level to *richard* and then back down to *jack*.

### 2.4   A Survey of File Handling Commands

Now lets look at some of the other file-handling commands in UNIX. First we will create another file in *john*.

```
$ cd
$ pwd
/user/richard
```

## Comparing files

These commands make sure we are in the home directory. The *cd* command without an argument after it has the effect of putting you back in your home directory: *pwd* checks that you are there. Let us now copy another file:

```
$ cp file2 john/file3
```

We now have two files in *john*. Let us compare them using the command *cmp*.

```
$ cd john
$ cmp file2 file3
file2 file3 differ: char 116, line 5
```

This command tells us whether two files differ and, if so, the byte at which the first difference occurs. Here the difference first occurs right at the end, on the last byte in fact, where *file2* has the added period.

## Common Line Finder

A command which compares two files and which tells us rather more about them is *comm*. We do:

```
$ comm file2 file3
                This is the first line
                This is the second line
                This is the third line
                This is the fourth line
        This is the last line
  This is the last line.
```

The *comm* command compares and prints the two files, justifying the printout to the right if the lines are the same in both files and printing out further to the left for differences; the lines which differ are printed in a position corresponding to the order in which the files were specified to the command.

## Finding differences

Another command which compares files and notes differences between them is *diff*.

```
$ diff file2 file3
5c5
< This is the last line.
---
> This is the last line
```

The output of *diff* is first of all a series of lines in the form of numbers around the letter 'a', 'c' or 'd', followed by the lines which need to be changed to make the files the same. These can be interpreted as *commandes to ed* to change *file2* into *file3*. Indeed you could redirect the output of the *diff* command to the editor and it would do the job.

This illustrates the interconnected nature of UNIX commands. As we will see later, commands are often designed so that they can used together, sometimes in a single line.

## 2.5 Some Simple Commands

We shall now look at some examples of simpler commands in UNIX. This will give a good idea of the flavour of working in the operating system. More advanced utilities will be considered in Chapter 6. The commands which follow are considered purely in alphabetical order.

### *ac* (keeping account)

The accounting command, *ac*, gives a detailed record of the login time spent by each user of the UNIX system. If used with the option 'p' it will list individual totals for the period covered by the current contents of the file /usr/adm/wtmp:

```
$ ac -p
        root      53.10
        mark       2.71
        xqa2      13.30
        xjd1     114.71
        egb9       1.11
        jpa        2.75
        jgbh      20.24
        clj6       0.18
```

```
alan        1.95
clj4       12.69
cla9        0.50
bob         0.13
peter       2.92
xjd3        0.09
harry       0.11
judith      1.19
qci8       10.30
richard     3.34
clive       0.05
xqd9        2.11
dick       12.66
xqd1        4.15
lauer       2.13
xqd3        2.03
pete       20.99
xqd2        0.64
xqd7        6.45
ega2        2.10
xqe1        0.07
lyn         0.05
xqd8        0.03
qci1        0.52
qci7       40.25
egc1        2.42
xqd6        0.14
cle7        4.87
total     343.36
```

## *deroff*   (removing roff constructs)

The command   *deroff* is used in conjunction with the   *roff* suite of formatting commands.  *roff* is treated in more detail later in Chapter 6. All we need note here is that *roff* works by using formatting constructs which are embedded in the text by the user. For instance the construct:

    **.fi n**

produces  *n*  blank lines when the text is processed by  *roff.*

    **.ti n**

gives a temporary indent of  *n* spaces from the left hand margin of the page.

    **.fi**

is an instruction to  *fill* lines, that is, to take words and pack them into the required line length. There are many other such constructs, which enable the user to produce a prettily formatted document with very little extra effort. The function of the *deroff* command is to strip the *roff* constructs from such a prepared text (perhaps prior to doing a statistical analysis of the content.) To show how it works, we will first produce a 'roffed' text:

```
$ ed
a
.jo
.ti 5
The wealth of nations is a subject
seriously studied by many,
economists and political theorists not least.
The conclusions which they have
drawn concerning this intractable subject
are as diverse as the disciplines of
the students themselves,
and the practicability of their solutions
is of the same order as the likelihood
of their proponents reaching agreement.
.
w adam
124
q
```

This text, if passed through *roff*, might look like this:

```
    The wealth of nations is a subject seriously studied
by many, economists and political theorists not least.
The conclusions which they have drawn concerning this
intractable subject are as diverse as the disciplines
of the students themselves, and the practicability of
their solutions is of the same order as the likelihood
of their proponents reaching agreement.
```

We will now de-roff the text:

```
$ deroff adam
The wealth of nations is a subject
seriously studied by many,
economists and political theorists not least.
The conclusions which they have
drawn concerning this intractable subject
are as diverse as the disciplines of
the students themselves,
and the practicability of their solutions
is of the same order as the likelihood
of their proponents reaching agreement.
```

## *diff3*  (three way diff)

We have already seen the use of the differential file comparator  *diff.*
There is also a 3-way differential file comparator, which compares three
versions of the 'same' file and prints out flagged disagreements
between them.
   We have three such files: file1, file2 and file3. First we'll make sure we
are in the home directory:

```
$ cd
$ diff3 file1 john/file2 john/file3
====2
1:5c
2:5c
   This is the last line.
3:5c
   This is the last line
```

   This print out means that file 2 (file2 in directory *john*) is different from
the others, and that the files can be made the same in one of two ways:
either by changing file 2:line 5 to read 'This is the last line.', or by
changing file 3:line 5 to read 'This is the last line'.


## *file*  (find file type)

The *file* command is a facility for finding the filetype of the file specified.
The command works all right with some filetypes, not so well with
others, as may be seen:

```
$ file file1
file1:   commands text
$ file ecec
ecec:    commands text
$ file john
john:    directory
$ file .
 .:      directory
$ file xx
xx:      cannot stat
```

   In general,  *file* overestimates the frequency of command files.


## *join*  (relational database operator)

The relational database operator,  *join*, performs the operation of
logically joining two files. This means that a 'join field' is specified (by

25

default the join field is the first field of each line) and a line of output is generated for each pair of lines which have that join field in common. The output line consists of the join field followed by the rest of the line in file2 and then the rest of the line in file3. For instance, if we join the two files *file2* and *file3*, we get:

```
$ join file2 file3
This is the first line is the first line
This is the first line is the second line
This is the first line is the third line
This is the first line is the fourth line
This is the first line is the last line
This is the second line is the first line
This is the second line is the second line
This is the second line is the third line
This is the second line is the fourth line
This is the second line is the last line
This is the third line is the first line
This is the third line is the second line
This is the third line is the third line
This is the third line is the fourth line
This is the third line is the last line
This is the fourth line is the first line
This is the fourth line is the second line
This is the fourth line is the third line
This is the fourth line is the fourth line
This is the fourth line is the last line
This is the last line. is the first line
This is the last line. is the second line
This is the last line. is the third line
This is the last line. is the fourth line
This is the last line. is the last line
```

## *ln* (link a file)

A *link* between two directories can be made by means of the *ln* command. First we examine the home directory:

```
$ cd
$ ls -l
total 42
-rwxrwxr-x 1 richard     5838 Apr 15 10:47 a.out
-rw-rw-r-- 1 richard       57 Apr  8 17:38 avesal.c
-rw-rw-r-- 1 richard      186 Apr 17 21:42 convert.c
-rw-rw-r-- 1 richard     9344 Apr 17 21:43 core
-rwx------ 1 richard       77 Mar 14 11:17 ecec
-rw-rw-r-- 1 richard      166 Apr 14 20:31 ed.hup
-rwx------ 1 richard       15 Mar 16 16:03 esp
```

```
-rw-------  1 richard     117 Mar 16 15:54 ex
-rw-rw-r--  1 richard      31 Apr  8 17:32 hello.c
drwx------  3 richard      96 Apr 13 20:27 john
-rw-rw-r--  1 richard     492 Mar 24 20:47 poeml
-rw-rw-r--  1 richard      59 Apr 15 10:39 test.c
-rwxrwxrwx  1 richard     116 Mar  9 20:01 file1
```

If we now want to link the file *file2* in directory *john*, we do a *ln* command and then inspect the directory again:

```
$ ln john/file2
$ ls -l
total 43
-rwxrwxr-x  1 richard    5838 Apr 15 10:47 a.out
-rw-rw-r--  1 richard      57 Apr  8 17:38 avesal.c
-rw-rw-r--  1 richard     186 Apr 17 21:42 convert.c
-rw-rw-r--  1 richard    9344 Apr 17 21:43 core
-rwx------  1 richard      77 Mar 14 11:17 ecec
-rw-rw-r--  1 richard     166 Apr 14 20:31 ed.hup
-rwx------  1 richard      15 Mar 16 16:03 esp
-rw-------  1 richard     117 Mar 16 15:54 ex
-rw-rw-r--  1 richard      31 Apr  8 17:32 hello.c
-rwx------  2 richard     117 Mar  9 20:14 file2
drwx------  3 richard      96 Apr 13 20:27 john
-rw-rw-r--  1 richard     492 Mar 24 20:47 poeml
-rw-rw-r--  1 richard      59 Apr 15 10:39 test.c
-rwxrwxrwx  1 richard     116 Mar  9 20:01 file1
```

Notice that *file2* now appears as an entry in the home directory, and that its 'link' field (the first numeral) has the value 2, having previously had a link count of 1.


## look   (find lines in a file)

We can find lines in a sorted file with the command   *look*. This command will print all lines which begin with the specified field:

```
$ sort file1 >temp
$ look -df this temp
This is the first line
This is the fourth line
This is the last line
This is the second line
This is the third line
```

The flag -d means search in 'dictionary' order: the flag -f means 'fold'; i.e. treat upper case and lower case characters as equivalent.

## *man*   (on-line manual)

There is an on-line manual available to UNIX users which will print out
sections of itself if the command  *man*  is given specifying the title of
the section you want and, if required, the chapter as well. If the chapter
is omitted, all sections with that title will be printed: e.g.

```
$ man wc

WC(1)                    Unix Programmer's Manual                    WC(1)

NAME
       wc - word count

SYNOPSIS
       wc [ -lwc ] [ name ... ]

DESCRIPTION
       Wc counts lines,  words and characters in the named
       files, or in the standard input if no name appears.
       A word is a maximal  string of characters delimited
       by spaces, tabs  or  newlines.

       If the optional argument is present, just the spec-
       ified counts  (lines,  words  or  characters)  are
       selected by the letters l, w, or c.

Printed 4/18/87
```

## *mv* (change a filename)

Files can be 'moved' (renamed) by the  *mv* command:

```
$ ls -l
total 44
-rw-rw-r-- 1 richard          57 Apr  8 17:38 avesal.c
-rw-rw-r-- 1 richard         186 Apr 17 21:42 convert.c
-rwx------ 1 richard          77 Mar 14 11:17 ecec
-rwx------ 1 richard          15 Mar 16 16:03 esp
-rw------- 1 richard         117 Mar 16 15:54 ex
-rw-rw-r-- 1 richard          31 Apr  8 17:32 hello.c
-rwx------ 2 richard         117 Mar  9 20:14 file2
drwx------ 3 richard          96 Apr 13 20:27 john
-rw-rw-r-- 1 richard         492 Mar 24 20:47 poem1
-rw-rw-r-- 1 richard         116 Apr 18 12:10 temp
-rw-rw-r-- 1 richard          59 Apr 15 10:39 test.c
```

28

```
-rwxrwxrwx 1 richard      116 Mar  9 20:01 file1
$ mv file1 textfile02
$ ls -1
total 44
-rw-rw-r-- 1 richard       57 Apr  8 17:38 avesal.c
-rw-rw-r-- 1 richard      186 Apr 17 21:42 convert.c
-rwx------ 1 richard       77 Mar 14 11:17 ecec
-rwx------ 1 richard       15 Mar 16 16:03 esp
-rw------- 1 richard      117 Mar 16 15:54 ex
-rw-rw-r-- 1 richard       31 Apr  8 17:32 hello.c
drwx------ 3 richard       96 Apr 13 20:27 john
-rw-rw-r-- 1 richard      492 Mar 24 20:47 poem1
-rw-rw-r-- 1 richard      116 Apr 18 12:10 temp
-rw-rw-r-- 1 richard       59 Apr 15 10:39 test.c
-rwxrwxrwx 1 richard      116 Mar  9 20:01 file1
-rwx------ 2 richard      117 Mar  9 20:14 textfile02
```

## *mail*   (electronic mail)

In UNIX you can write to your friends on the system with the *mail* command:

```
$ mail egc1
Dear Graeme,
          Long time no mail. How are things?
                   Yours,
                       Richard.
```

The text is inserted following the same conventions as for the editor *ed*, and is terminated by a period.

If there is mail for you, you are told about it when you log in:

```
login: richard
password:
You have mail.
$
```

## *nice*   (being nice to others)

The command *nice* runs another command at a low priority:

```
$ nice -10 date
Tue May 11 19:34:27 BST 1982
```

The difference is not, of course, perceptible to the naked eye. The effect is that the command does not hog processor time (see Chapter 5).

## *nm* (symbol table listing)

The *nm* command is used to produce a symbol table for object files. Suppose, for example, that we have a program written in the language C (see Chapter 5). To turn it into an object file we run the C compiler with the *cc* command. The object file is placed by default in a file called *a.out*. We can then produce a symbol table, of which only the first few lines are shown by way of example:

```
$ cc avesal.c
$ nm a.out
000021 a .break
000006 a .close
000066 a .ioctl
000004 a .write
002316 T cleanu
000204 T doprnt
001632 T flsbuf
004356 D iob
004616 D lastbu
005644 B sibuf
004644 B sobuf
001332 T strout
006654 b allocp
006650 b allocs
006656 b alloct
006660 b allocx
004040 T brk
003672 T close
006664 B end
006646 B environ
006644 B errno
002516 T exit
002354 T fclose
etc.
```

...the full symbol table contains another 120 lines.

## *od* (octal dump)

The dump command *od* can be used to produce a file dump in one of a number of formats. The .bo c .xb option produces ASCII characters corresponding to the bytes of the file, with special characters represented by escape sequences beginning with '\':

```
$ od -c temp
0000000   (  e   x   e   c      $   a            t   e   e   t
```

```
0000020    e    m    p    1    )   \n    c    a    t         t    e    m    p         >
0000040    >    p    e    r    m   \n    c    a    t         t    e    m    p    1   \n
0000060    c    a    t         t    e    m    p    1         >    >    p    e    r    m
0000100   \n    c    h    m    o    d         +    x         t    e    m    p   \n    d
0000120    o   \n    d    o    n    e   \n    e    c    h    o         $    a         >
0000140    t    e    m    p   \n    e    c    h    o         -    n         '    £
0000160    '   \n    e    c    h    o         -    n         '    £         '   \n    e
0000200    c    h    o         -    n         '    $         '         >    >    p    e
0000220    r    m   \n    r    e    a    d         a   \n    r    e    a    d         a
0000240   \n    w    h    i    l    e         t    e    s    t         -    n         $
0000260    a   \n
0000262
```

When used with the flag -b, the *od* command produces a dump in octal:

```
$ od -b temp
0000000 050 145 170 145 143 040 044 141 040 174 040 164 145 145 040 164
0000020 145 155 160 061 051 012 143 141 164 040 164 145 155 160 040 076
0000040 076 160 145 162 155 012 143 141 164 040 164 145 155 160 061 012
0000060 143 141 164 040 164 145 155 160 061 040 076 076 160 145 162 155
0000100 012 143 150 155 157 144 040 053 170 040 164 145 155 160 012 144
0000120 157 012 144 157 156 145 012 145 143 150 157 040 044 141 040 076
0000140 164 145 155 160 012 145 143 150 157 040 055 156 040 047 043 040
0000160 047 012 145 143 150 157 040 055 156 040 047 043 040 047 012 145
0000200 143 150 157 040 055 156 040 047 044 040 047 040 076 076 160 145
0000220 162 155 012 162 145 141 144 040 141 012 162 145 141 144 040 141
0000240 012 167 150 151 154 145 040 164 145 163 164 040 055 156 040 044
0000260 141 012
0000262
```

And the flag -x produces hexadecimal:

```
$ od -x temp
0000000 6528 6578 2063 6124 7c20 7420 6565 7420
0000020 6d65 3170 0a29 6163 2074 6574 706d 3e20
0000040 703e 7265 0a6d 6163 2074 6574 706d 0a31
0000060 6163 2074 6574 706d 2031 3e3e 6570 6d72
0000100 630a 6d68 646f 2b20 2078 6574 706d 640a
0000120 0a6f 6f64 656e 650a 6863 206f 6124 3e20
0000140 6574 706d 650a 6863 206f 6e2d 2720 2023
0000160 0a27 6365 6f68 2d20 206e 2327 2720 650a
0000200 6863 206f 6e2d 2720 2024 2027 3e3e 6570
0000220 6d72 720a 6165 2064 0a61 6572 6461 6120
0000240 770a 6968 656c 7420 7365 2074 6e2d 2420
0000260 0a61
0000262
```

## *Passwd* (changing your password)

You can change your password if you wish to (and it is wise to do so from time to time on security grounds) by means of the *passwd* command. The command asks for the old password and then for the new password, which it asks to have repeated, to avoid possible errors. The following dialogue may appear rather sparse, as the passwords are not, of course, echoed on the terminal:

```
$ passwd
Changing password for bsu6
Old password:
New password:
Retype new password:
```

## *rm* (removing a file)

If you want to get rid of files use the *rm* command. This will remove the name from the directory as well as emptying the file contents. If you wake up in the night and wish you had the file back again, a file can sometimes be recovered by the system manager, but it is best not to count on it.

## *rmdir* (remove directory)

This should be used for removing directories, which must first be empty. If you want to remove a non-empty directory it may first be emptied by using the form:

```
$ rmdir -r <directory>
```

This will empty the directory and any files (or directories) in it. It may involve a long descent of the tree, and should only be used if you are absolutely certain there is nothing there you want.

## *stty* (set terminal characteristics)

The characteristics of the terminal which you are using may be altered by means of the command *stty*. For instance, the terminal can be set to cope with even or odd parity, to echo or suppress echo, to set tab stops and to allocate characters to particular functions, such as erase, kill and interrupt (break). In the following example, the flag '-echo' is used, turning off the echo at the terminal.

```
$ stty -echo
$ command: not found
$ $
```

Following the *stty* command, another command 'command' was given, but not echoed. Since there is no command 'command' the shell replied with an error message, which did print. The command 'stty echo' was then given, turning on the echo again.

## *tail* (getting hold of the tail)

The command *tail* will yield the 'tail', or last part of a file. The number of lines, blocks or characters to be printed are specified:

```
$ tail -31 file1
This is the third line
This is the fourth line
This is the last line
```

## *tee* (a joint in a pipe)

The command *tee* copies the input to the output, copying it also to a file:

```
$ tee -a teefile.t
Here is a line of input
Here is a line of input
Here is another
Here is another
$ cat teefile.t
Here is a line of input
Here is another
```

## *time* (telling the time)

Commands can be timed by means of the command *time*, which prints the time elapsed during the command, the time spent by the user and the time spent by the system in executing the command, all in units of seconds:

```
$ time date
Mon May 17 20:26:25 BST 1987

real         1.0
user         0.0
sys          0.3
```

## touch   (putting the finger on a file)

If you want to update the last access to a file without altering the file itself, this can be done by means of the command *touch*, which works by reading one character of the file and then rewriting it to the file:

```
$ ls -l avesal.c
-rwx------ 1 bsu6        57 Apr  8 17:38 avesal.c
$ touch avesal.c
$ ls -l avesal.c
-rwx------ 1 bsu6        57 May 17 20:27 avesal.c
```

## tr   (translate)

The *tr* command is a powerful way of translating input by substitution. Two strings can be specified, the characters of the first string being replaced by those of the second whenever they occur:

```
$ tr line bear
This is line one
Thes es bear oar
How do you do?
How do you do?
```

## tty   (find out who you are)

The *tty* command tells you the name of the terminal you are using:

```
$ tty
/dev/tty02
```

## uniq   (find duplicate lines)

The command *uniq* finds duplicate lines in files. It will report either the unique lines or the repeated lines, depending on the flag specified. To demonstrate its use we must first create a file with duplicate lines:

```
$ ed dup
?dup
a
This is line one
This is line one
This is the last line
.
w
56
q
```

Now, using the default option we get unique lines:

```
$ uniq dup
This is line one
This is the last line
```

Or, with the flag -d, we get the duplicate lines:

```
$ uniq -d dup
This is line one
```

So much for the first rapid survey of some of UNIX's facilities. It is hoped that this has given a flavour of the use of the system. In the next chapter we shall look at the UNIX file system in more detail.

# 3 The UNIX File System

## 3.1 File Structure

The treatment of files in the UNIX system is very straightforward. In many ways it is a simplification of the file structures required by other systems, and imposes no demands on the user as far as contents or layout of the file are concerned. Nor are there any requirements for record counts, hash totals or other checking procedures. If these are needed, they may be added by the user, but they do not form part of the operating system itself.

Similarly, any structure which may be needed in files can be introduced by the user, who is not restricted to conventions such as eighty-character records. It may seem at first as though this is a reduction in the available facilities, but this is far from being the case. Any desired file structure is still available to the user: however, it is a matter for the user's software and not the operating system. Also, this way of dealing with files has considerable advantages in other ways, allowing uniformity of addressing and free communication between commands.

A UNIX file is a series of bytes, each byte containing one item of information, which may be a digit, letter or other character in ASCII (American Standard Code for Information Interchange) code, or may be in binary or some other representation. The internal organisation of a file is of no consequence to UNIX. In computer science terms, a UNIX file is a one-dimensional byte array. For general purposes, this is the only structure assumed in a file by UNIX.

Even different file types are of limited interest to the system, a directory being for many purposes just another file. A special feature of UNIX is that input and output devices are also treated as files: reading from a file which is an input device results in the device being read, and conversely writing into such a file causes a write to the device. (The resulting operations are not necessarily physical read or write operations.)

This uniform treatment of files is of considerable value to the system, enabling a great deal of intercommunication between files, and also allowing a good deal of standardisation in the command structure. As we shall see, it is one of the main strengths of UNIX as an operating system.

## 3.2 The File System

The UNIX file system does, however, have an external structure. This is the hierarchical or tree-like form of the file system, shown both in the files maintained by the UNIX system itself, and those set up at the discretion of the user. This tree-like structure of the file system makes the storage and retrieval of files a more economical proposition, both for the system and from the point of view of the user.

Certain commands in UNIX treat a file as being subdivided into *lines*, one line being separated from another by a special character called a newline character (or its equivalent for certain purposes, the sequence of carriage return and line feed characters). The purpose of dividing a file into lines is to allow editing of files. As we have seen, files can be created, amended and deleted as required by the *ed* command. *ed* works on a line-by-line basis, and distinguishes the line boundaries by means of the newline character.

Certain other commands also operate on files in a line-by-line manner, for example the *rev* command, which copies the input file to the output file, reversing the order of the bytes in each line as it does so, or the *uniq* command, which reports on repeated lines in a file. It remains true, however, that to the system as a whole, a file is simply a series of bytes about whose structure it knows nothing except how many of them there are. (Byte counts are maintained and used by many commands, and are vital data for UNIX.)

## 3.3 File Types

From the user's point of view there are three distinct kinds of file in UNIX: these are ordinary files, directories and special files. We shall look at each of these in some detail.

### Ordinary files

The internal structure of ordinary files has already been discussed: there is no structure beyond the division of the file into lines for certain purposes. Externally, ordinary files are stored on disk in a random access fashion: that is, the information can be retrieved from any part of the file as easily as from any other.

## The i-list

Disks are divided up into blocks of 512 bytes each. The first block (block 0) is not used for file storage by the system. Block 1 is the 'super-block', and this contains information about the size of the file areas held on the rest of the disk. Subsequent blocks hold the *i-list*, which is a list of file definitions. The rest of the disk contains the areas which are available for the files themselves.

The i-list consist of file definitions, called i-nodes. The name 'nodes' suggests that the structure of the file system is like a tree, and the files correspond to nodes on the tree.

Each file is known by a number in the i-list, called the i-number of the file. This is an important piece of information about the file, and it is needed both by the system and at times by the user, for example when dealing with files during system checks by the super-user (see Chapter 7).

Besides the i-number, the i-node contains other information relating to the file. The i-node is 64 bytes in length and contains all information relating to a file from the system's purposes. The user does not need to know the contents of the i-node of the files he is using, but the i-node contains the information necessary to tell the system where on the disk the file is located.

## Link counts

The i-node contains a record called the link-count, which shows the number of directories the file appears in. When a file is created it is assigned an i-node, and the corresponding i-number is stored in the directory of the creator of the file. If any other link is made to the file, it will be entered in the directory to which the new link is made. The i-node will also be amended to record the fact that the file has entries in two directories and the link-count will be incremented by one.

When a file is deleted from a directory, its i-number is deleted from that directory and the link-count is reduced by one. If the link-count field becomes zero, the file is assumed to have no remaining users and its disk areas are freed for other files to occupy. This constitutes deletion of a file.

## File storage

Besides the link-count, the i-node also contains a series of 13 disk addresses, which specify the file's location on the disk. These are implemented in three stages in a system designed to accommodate files of different sizes.

The first 10 addresses point directly to the first 10 blocks of the file. The eleventh address points to a disk block which in turn contains the addresses of up to 128 further blocks of the file, if required. If the file is larger than this, then the twelfth address of the i-node contains the address of a block which contains the addresses of a further 128 blocks, each of which contains the addresses of 128 blocks of the file.

This will cope with files up to 8 459 264 bytes in size. Larger files than this use the thirteenth address of the i-node to address up to 1 082 201 087 bytes by an extension of the process through three stages of indirect addressing. This deals with all but the largest files.

This method of storage means that access to file areas depends on the part of the file which they occupy. Files less than 5120 bytes in length can be read with a single disk access. Files between 5120 and 70 656 bytes in size require two disk accesses, and so on. This is quite an efficient process for most purposes, but time is saved wherever possible in the UNIX system by keeping files in memory if they are going to be used again soon (for example if they are shared between two or more users of the system).

Not all the files in a single file system need to be physically held on one disk. Disks may be attached or detached from the system at will, by means of the system requests *mount* and *umount*. The request to *mount* results in the disk being attached to the system with the root directory specified in *mount*. The files on the disk which has been mounted then become part of the tree available to the user.


## System checks

Although the user need not concern himself with the contents of the i-node of a file, he may need to know its i-number, especially when checking the validity of the file system after something has gone wrong. The i-number is used to identify each file to the system, and certain system maintenance commands need the i-number to work with. However, these commands are not available to all users of a UNIX system: they may only be used by the priveleged user(s) of that system – the super-user. The use of these commands will be covered in Chapter 7.

## File access

Reading and writing files is carried out in sequential fashion: that is to say, after a read or write operation the next read or write refers to the next byte of the file.

As has been suggested, files may be accessed by more than one user at the same time, and it might be thought that this could lead to problems of garbling of information, interference between users and so on. The answer is that important files (e.g. system files) can be read but not, in general, written to. Where two or more users share their own files they can probably sort out such problems for themselves more easily than having system-imposed restrictions on simultaneous access. At any rate, generic UNIX does not impose any such file locks on users.

## Directories

The concept of the UNIX directory is at the heart of the UNIX file system. A directory is, for most user purposes, simply a read-only file, which contains information about the files within it. All active files appear as an entry in some directory, and some appear in more than one directory.

Directories are maintained by the system in a tree-like structure of branches and sub-branches. At the bottom of the tree there is a directory known as the *root*. Any permitted file may be found by a search in the correct sequence through the tree, beginning, if necessary, at the root.

## File permission

Files which are not permitted may not be read, written or executed depending on the nature of the access allowed.

For file access purposes there are three groups of users. These are: the user (u), members of the same group as the user (g) and any others (o).

Access to members of these three groups is decided by the file's owner. Access is controlled by means of bits called permission bits in the directory. These bits and permissions may be set using the *chmod* command (see p. 44).

## Pathnames

The sequence necessary to access a file is known as its *pathname*. Pathnames are sequences of names separated by the slash character '/'.

If the pathname begins with a '/' character then the search starts in the root. If it does not start with a '/' then the search begins in the current directory the user is in – not necessarily the home directory.

## Home directory

The home directory for each user is a subdirectory in a directory called */usr*. When you login you are automatically in your home directory, which may for example be called *richard*. Its full pathname is thus */usr/ richard*. The pathname */usr/richard/file01* causes a search in the root directory for the directory *usr* and then searches *usr* for *richard* and finally *richard* for *file01*.

A path name is thus a series of names separated by slashes, the final one being the name of the required file, and the others (if any) being the names of directories. (This illustrates quite well the equivalence for many purposes of file and directory names.) A single filename by itself expects to be found in the current directory. A slash by itself specifies the root.

## File system structure

The structure of the file system has already been mentioned. This is one point in which ordinary files and directories are differently treated. Directories must conform strictly to the tree-like structure: no directory may be an entry in more than one other directory. Ordinary files on the other hand may have several entries in different directories.

This is because otherwise the amount of checking the system would have to do when a directory was emptied before allowing it to be deleted would be too large to handle conveniently.

Another restriction which should be noticed is that links cannot be created between files on two devices if one of them can be dismounted. Also, a directory cannot be split between two or more devices.

## Parent and child directories

The symbols '.' and '..' have special meanings in relation to directories. They refer to the directory itself and to its 'parent', that is, the directory which created it. So, for example, to say

    cd ..

results in the parent of the directory you are in becoming the working directory.
    Saying

    cd .

would not change the working directory, since '.' specifies the current directory.
    These two special symbols are found as entries in all directories, (except for the root, which has no parent, and hence no '..' entry). These directory entries can be displayed by using the command *ls -a*. Without the use of the 'a' option the entries beginning with '.' are normally suppressed.

## Special files

An unusual and valuable feature of UNIX is its treatment of devices. A device is known by a name which has the same appearance as a file name, and which takes its place in the hierarchy of the file system. This applies to any input or output device, and means that devices can be addressed in the same way as files.
    There is no apparent distinction between the handling of devices which may be used for both input and output, such as disks, and those which can be used for input only, such as readers, or those which can be used for output only, like a punch (requests which are not appropriate to a particular type of device will, of course, be refused by the system).
    Device names for the system are kept in the directory */dev*. To write or read a device you specify the device name as it appears in this directory. A printer might, for example, be known as *ptr*, and it would be addressed as */dev/ptr*. Memory may also be treated as a device, and

portions of addressable memory may have device names which will be found in */dev*.

The advantages of this way of treating devices are considerable. It means, firstly, that the system can easily allow the user to interchange device names and file names, to attach devices to the system as required, and to keep device details in the same format as it keeps file details and directory details. This preserves uniformity within the system.

The other reason for this way of treating files, directories and devices is more complex. Since devices can be treated in the same way as files, communication between commands, system requests and other programs can be made much easier.

In UNIX, the output of one command can be made the input to another by means of a mechanism called a 'pipe' (see Chapter 4). Using pipes, files can be linked together, and streams of input and output can be rerouted with facility. None of this would be so easy if it were not for the fact that file, directory and device names take the same form and can be replaced with one another.

## 3.4  Redirection

One of the powerful features of UNIX is the ability of the user to redirect the input and output from programs to any file he wishes. The standard destination for output is the user's own terminal, and in many cases this will be what is wanted.

For example, when asking for a listing of a directory, the command

```
ls -l
```

will produce the listing on the terminal. If this listing is required in a file instead of for immediate inspection, this can be got by giving the command

```
ls -l > outfile
```

The file following the '>' sign becomes the output file for the duration of the *ls* command.

Similarly, giving the command

```
ls -l >> outfile
```

causes the output of the *ls* command to be appended to *outfile*. In the first example it would replace the contents of *outfile*, if any.

This is an example of the redirection of output from one file to another. The terminal (which is itself a special file) was assumed to be the destination of the command's output. When a new output file was specified the output was sent there instead.

## Input redirection

Input files can be redirected as well as output files. The input to a command is assumed to come from the terminal, if no other source is specified. However another file (or special file) can be made the input by using the symbol '<', which makes the file whose name follows the sign become the standard input for the duration of the command.

For instance, the command

```
ed < infile
```

will run the editor and take its commands from *infile*, rather than from the terminal. In other words, *infile* is interpreted as a stream of commands to the editor and the result is printed on the terminal.

It will be appreciated that in redirecting files in this way it is necessary for UNIX to be able to replace files with devices and vice versa.

## 3.5 File Security

The UNIX system is well supplied with means to protect the security of your file system. Security means a number of things.

First, it means that you do not want unauthorised people looking at your files, for whatever reason.

Second, it implies that you may want to deny permission to others to do certain things with your files (or conversely, you may want to permit them to do certain things). For example, you may decide to allow others to read, but not write to your files.

Third, it means the existence of safeguards against losing your data, either through your own accident or someone else's design (this includes safeguarding the system against crashes due to your own or someone else's misdeeds).

All these security features are accomplished by the UNIX system of file protection.

## Permissions

Each file in the UNIX file system is provided with a set of bits which give or withold permission to do certain things with that file, set by means of the *chmod* command. There are three types of permission; read, write and execute, and these can be applied to three groups of users, the user himself, people in the same group and people other than these.

The read permission bit allows the file to be read, the write bit allows the file to be altered by writing information to it and the execute bit lets you execute the file (in the case of program files).

Setting each of these bits permits the relevant function to be carried out independently of the others.

For example you might decide that you wanted to read information from a file but not write to it (perhaps because you are afraid of losing the data). This could be done by setting the read bits, but not the write bits. Later you might decide that you wanted to change the information in the file (perhaps because you now had a copy of it), in which case the write permission bits could now be turned on.

Execute permission could be witheld, for example, from a program file until you were sure that it would cause no harm if the program were run. Only the owner of the file (with one exception, that of the super-user) can set or reset these permission bits.

## Group permissions

In addition, these permissions can be given to the three different groups of users. There is a set of read, write and execute bits which apply to the owner only, another set of permission bits which apply to other users in the same user group as the owner of the file and a set of permission bits which apply to all other users.

By means of these different groups of bits it is possible to set up flexible arrangements for the use allowed for a given file. For instance, you might decide to allow others in the same user group to read or execute a program file, but only permit other users to execute it without accessing the source code, while still retaining the ability to amend the program yourself.

## Permitting directories

In the case of a directory, the meaning of the permission bits is somewhat altered. To 'read' means to be able to inspect the names of files in the directory, while 'write' means the ability to write to files in the directory, a permission which extends control beyond the immediate confines of the directory file itself.

The meaning of 'execute' is also somewhat different in the case of a directory, where it means the ability to search for a given file in the directory. Again, the permission bits are grouped by the class of user, but only the owner may change these bits.

## 3.6 File Handling Commands

Having discussed the file system in some detail, and gained an appreciation of how it works, let us now look at some of the commands used in handling files. Some of these commands have already been mentioned in outline in Chapter 2, but here a fuller treatment of them will be given in order to enable the reader to understand their method of operation and effect in some detail. Some of the commands which maintain files and which give diagnostic information about their position in the file system are only available to those with super-user status (see Chapter 7) and will be discussed elsewhere.

### Creating files – the text editor

The most fundamental way of getting information to a file is via the text editor. The command *ed* invokes the editor which then awaits commands. If the command specifies a name, then a file of that name is looked for first in the current directory, since the editor presumes first that it is being asked to operate on an existing file. However, if no file with that name is found then a warning '?' is printed with the name.

The name is not forgotten, however, and if a *w* command is given later on, then a file of that name will be created and the information in the edited file will be written to it. The *ed* command in fact works by simulating an *e* command which is available within the text editor. It is better to avoid the error message altogether, when editing a new file, by using the sequence:

```
$ ed e name
```

### Text buffer

The text editor operates on a temporary file or *buffer* in which the information in the file is held during the editing. Since the temporary file is a copy of the file you are editing, then the original is preserved. If an existing file is being edited, then no change is made to it until a *w* operation takes place. The buffer can be added to, deleted, searched or changed using the *ed* commands.

## *Regular expressions*

The editor works on the principle of modifying strings of characters within a line: such strings are accessed by means of what is known as 'regular expressions'. A regular expression is a way of specifying one or more strings which conform to your requirements, and includes rules such as 'The character ".ic" matches any character', and 'a regular expression preceded by the character " " matches only strings that begin at the left of a line'. The rules for forming regular expressions are set out at more length in Chapter 6.

## *Output*

When all the emendations have been carried out then the command *w* causes the new file to be written. No backup file is automatically provided, as in some editors, so if you want backup files you must write to a new file name each time you do an editing operation.

Editing is carried out on lines, rather than on free areas of text in the buffer, and it can be less than straightforward to edit across more than one line, although there are ways of specifying the 'newline' character in searches. Lines are known by their sequential position in the buffer, and a line number is required by each command in *ed*, even though the default value is often adequate.

The editor also uses the concept of the 'current line'. It always assumes that it is operating on a line with a given number, usually the last one addressed by the previous command. The current line does not change unless some command is carried out which changes it explicitly.

The editor's limitations are that it will not process lines longer than 512 characters, or commands in excess of 256 characters in length. The largest temporary file size it can handle is 128k characters which is, however, large enough for most purposes, larger files being partitioned appropriately.

## Listing files

The simplest way of listing a file is to use the *cat* command. This is a command for copying files from one place to another, concatenating them (joining them end to end) if required. It can be used to copy a file to the terminal by default, if the output file is missing: in this way *cat* comes to be used as a 'list' command. (N.B. There is no command 'list', or any apparent equivalent mnemonic, a surprising omission to the first time user of UNIX.)

If the input is also missing then the command will wait for input from the terminal. A *cat* command without arguments will echo what has been put in at the terminal when 'endfile' is reached.

## Printing files

If a printed output is required, then the command *pr* should be used. This directs its output to the printer and provides paging of the output. At the top of each page a header is printed with the date and name of the file listed. The format of the printout can be specified by the arguments of the *pr* command: for example the width and length of the page can be specified, and new headings can be inserted. Several files can even be printed together in separate columns on the same page.

## Moving files

Files can be moved from one place to another by means of the *mv* command. This works effectively by renaming the file, which remains in the same place physically, unless the files are in different file-systems, in which case a copy must be made and a deletion carried out. If there is already a file with the destination name, then it is removed before the move is carried out. If the destination file exists and has a mode which forbids writing then the command issues a query enabling the user to override the mode. If he does so, then the new mode of the destination file is set to permit write by the owner and others of his group.

To copy a file to a destination, while preserving the original, the *cp* command is used. This will create a copy of the file under a new name: if the destination file already exists then it will be overwritten, providiing that write is permitted. If it is not, there is no way of overriding the mode setting. In order to copy groups of files the command *copy* can be used. This command enables you to copy whole directories if required, and to recursively descend any directories which may be found within a directory, copying their contents. In this way, whole file systems may be copied. The copy command makes use of links wherever it can: that is to say, a physical copy is not made unless it is necessary to do so. If copying across file systems, however, links cannot be used.

## Linking files

The linking of files can be otherwise achieved by means of the *ln* command. This sets up a directory entry in the destination directory which refers to the file which is the source. No physical copy need be made. From what has been said already about links it is apparent that this is an economical way of sharing files between different users. The number of links to a file is counted, and only when no further links exist can it be removed from the system.

## Comparing files

The facilities for manipulating the contents of files generally assume only that a file is divided into lines. The commands *cmp, comm* and *diff* can be used to compare two or more files and list either their common lines or differences. In the case of *diff* these differences are produced in such a form that they can be used as input to the *ed* command to make the two files the same.

## Sorting files

Files can be sorted into alphanumeric line sequence, and non-unique lines discarded by means of *sort* and *uniq*. If a further subdivision of the line is required the command *prep* will create a file with one word to each line. The use of these commands has given rise the classic UNIX one-liner:

```
prep afile | sort | uniq
```

which prints an alphabetic listing of the words used in *afile*. Database operations can be carried out by means of the relational database command *join* which performs the relational operation of logically joining two files together

## Maintaining files

The maintenance of the file system is provided for by a range of commands which enable the user to check for consistency, i-node numbering and disk space availability. Some of these commands are only accessible to the super-user, who as the 'manager' of the system is supposed to take the responsibility for checking the file system itself. These commands will be discussed in further detail in Chapter 7.

## 3.7 Mapping the File System

Although each UNIX installation has a slightly different file system, there tend to be common elements shared by all of them. By convention, UNIX utilities are kept in one set of files, object libraries in another, maintenance utilities in yet another and so on. It is possible, therefore, to generalise to some extent about file systems, and for this reason the user may profitably study such an 'idealised' file system hierarchy.

You should come to know where to find commands which are regularly used, commands which are occasionally used, details of user's facilities and records and so on. If you are the system manager it is particularly necessary to be able to find your way around the file system with the minimum of trouble. This section gives a succinct guide to the main features of such an 'idealised' file system, and shows how to find things in places where they might not have been expected.

### Root directory

The root of the file system is the directory /. A typical listing of / looks like this:

```
$ ls -l /
total 227
-rw-r--r--  1 root        105 Dec 22 14:14 .profile
drwxr-xr-x  2 bin        1904 Nov  8 12:04 bin
-rwxr--r--  1 root       8582 Jan 18  1982 boot
-rw-r--r--  1 root      36544 Dec 10 19:40 core
drwxr-xr-x  2 bin         960 Nov 18 17:16 dev
drwxr-xr-x  5 bin         672 Dec 20 16:10 etc
drwxr-xr-x  2 bin         480 Nov 13  1981 lib
drwxr-xr-x  8 root        128 Jul 26  1980 mnt
drwxr-xr-x  2 bin         160 Mar  1  1982 stand
drwxrwxrwx  2 root        416 Dec 31 01:21 tmp
-rwxr--r--  2 root      53738 Dec 22 14:15 unix
drwxr-xr-x41 sys        1200 Dec 29 19:58 user
drwxr-xr-x  2 root         32 Oct 12  1981 x
```

```
drwxrwxrwx24 root      416 Dec 14 15:25 y
drwxr-xr-x21 sys       464 Nov  9 11:40 z
```

You are now looking at the root of a tree-like structure which branches out from this directory into many other directories and files. The contents of / vary from one UNIX to another, but the above listing contains some of the most frequently found elements. The function of some of these files will now be explained.

## The *.profile* file

Every executable file in the above listing of / is itself a directory except for *boot, .profile* and *unix*. We will look at these latter two files first.

The file *.profile* is a file which contains commands which are to be executed at the time of system startup. The name *.profile* is not reserved for this purpose: however generally by convention a *.profile* file contains commands to be carried out when a given user logs in.

There is a *.profile* for the user *root* just as there is for other users, and it usually lists directly after '.' and '..' at the very start of the home directory. (That the files list in this way is a consequence of the collating sequence properties of ASCII characters.)

It is good practice for each user to maintain a *.profile* file in his home directory. It usually contains such things as the setting of the shell variable 'PATH' (the pathway to be searched for commands given to the shell) and 'MAIL' (the name of the file which contains mail for this user, though it can be used for many other purposes as well).

## UNIX system resident

The other non-directory file in / is the file called *unix*. This is the UNIX system resident, and is the file loaded when the system goes up initially or after a shutdown. In some systems there may be more than one version of the UNIX resident, configured to run from different hardware. In this case there may be various residents in / with names resembling one another. Care should be taken to use the right one at startup time!

## /bin

The rest of the files are themselves directories. The first of these, *bin*, holds the majority of the commands in the standard UNIX system, as the listing will show:

```
$ ls /bin
```

| | | | |
|---|---|---|---|
| ac | adb | ar | as |
| at | backup | basename | cat |
| cc | checktim | chgrp | chmod |
| chown | clri | cmp | comm |
| cp | cptree | cpv | date |
| dcheck | dcheck00 | dd | df |
| diff | diff3 | du | dump |
| dumpdir | echo | egrep | em |
| expr | false | fgrep | file |
| find | fsck | ft | grep |
| hardfp | icheck | info | iostat |
| ipatch | kill | ld | ln |
| login | logout | lorder | lpr |
| ls | lstree | mail | make |
| man | mkdir | mountbot | mountman |
| mv | ncheck | newgrp | nice |
| nm | nohup | od | oldpasswd |
| passwd | pr | ps | pstat |
| pwd | quot | ranlib | rkcmp |
| rkcp | rm | rmdir | rxfmt |
| sa | sc | sed | sepid |
| sh | shutdown | size | sleep |
| sort | spell | stopftp | strip |
| stty | su | suser | sync |
| tabs | tail | tee | test |
| testdate | time | touch | true |
| tty | umountbot | umountman | verify |
| wc | who | | |

## Search path

Naturally, the search path of most users as well as of *root* itself is set to include */bin*, so that any commands in this directory can be used without giving the full path name.

## /dev

The next directory to consider is *dev*. This holds the devices for the whole system. Each entry identifies the device type, its function and when it was last used, as well as giving the vitally important device number. A listing of */dev* might look like this:

```
$ ls -l /dev
total 5
crw------- 1 root     0,   1 Dec 31 12:02 console
```

```
crw-r--r--  1 bin       8,   1 Jul 26    1980 kmem
crw-------  1 daemon    6,   6 Dec 22 10:48 lp
-rw-r--r--  1 bin        2098 Jul 26    1980 makefile
crw-r--r--  1 bin       8,   0 Jul 26    1980 mem
crw-rw-rw-  1 bin       8,   2 Dec 23 13:23 null
brw-r--r--  1 root      0,   0 May 15    1982 rk0
brw-r--r--  1 root      0,   1 Mar 29    1982 rk1
brw-r--r--  1 root      0,   2 Nov  9    1981 rk2
brw-r--r--  1 root      0,   3 Nov 20    1981 rk3
brw-r--r--  1 root      0,   4 Oct 29 08:06 rk4
brw-r--r--  1 root      0,   5 Oct 29 08:06 rk5
brw-r--r--  1 root      0,   6 Feb 16    1981 rk6
brw-r--r--  1 root      0,   7 Nov 20    1981 rk7
brw-r--r--  1 root      9,   0 Mar 26    1981 rx0
brw-r--r--  1 root      9,   1 Feb 24    1981' rx1
brw-r--r--  1 root      9,   2 Jun  8    1981 ry0
brw-r--r--  1 root      9,   3 Feb 23    1981 ry1
crw--w--w-  1 richar    0,   1 Dec 31 12:10 tty01
crw--w--w-  1 root      0,   2 Dec 22 14:19 tty02
crw--w--w-  1 root      0,   3 Dec 22 14:19 tty03
crw--w--w-  1 root      0,   4 Dec 21 13:07 tty04
crw--w--w-  1 root      0,   5 Dec 17 15:44 tty05
crw--w--w-  1 root      0,   6 Dec 17 10:52 tty06
crw--w--w-  1 root      0,   7 Dec 17 10:54 tty07
crw--w--w-  1 root      0,   8 Dec 16 16:32 tty08
crw--w--w-  1 root      0,   9 Dec 16 16:24 tty09
crw--w--w-  1 root      0,  10 Dec 16 16:42 tty10
crw--w--w-  1 root      0,  11 Dec 16 12:59 tty11
crw--w--w-  1 root      0,  12 Dec 16 13:03 tty12
crw--w--w-  1 root      0,  13 Dec 16 13:03 tty13
crw--w--w-  1 root      0,  14 Dec 16 12:59 tty14
crw--w--w-  1 root      0,  15 Dec 16 13:03 tty15
```

As can be seen, each device has an entry in the directory /dev. The entry shows the date the device was created or last used, and its device name.

The first ten characters look very like the normal permission bits for a file, and they have here some of the same functions. The first character however is reserved for specifying the type of device. The character 'c' means a character-oriented device, that is, one which handles data as a stream of characters, like a terminal does. The character 'b' stands for a block-oriented device: devices such as floppy and hard disks are classified as block-oriented, since this is the way they handle their I/O.

The rest of the permission bits have the same meaning as for other files; that is they give the read, write and execute permissions for the user, members of his group and others who are not members of his group. In the case of devices, of course, the permissions to read and write must be appropriate for devices capable of input, output or both.

The next number printed for each entry is the number of links, as for normal file and directory listings. In each case the devices listed above have only one link. The next two numbers are the major and minor device number, and these specify the device uniquely to UNIX. For example, the teletype-like device *tty01* has the major device number 0 and minor device number 1, the device *tty02* has major 0 and and minor 2. These numbers are vital information to the system because they connect with the software device handlers which carry out the physical I/O for each device.

Note that apparent duplicate devices, i.e. those with the same major and minor device numbers, may exist under different names. For example, the device *console* may be major device number 0 and minor device number 0 and so may the device *tty01*. In this case the names are simply aliases for the same device.

Another case of apparent duplication may arise when the two devices are in fact of different I/O type, i.e. one of them is a character-type and the other a block-type file. Since the major and minor device numbers specify a device of a given type uniquely, there can be, by definition, only one device of that type with any such set of numbers.

Note also that memory appears as a device with the name here of *kmem*.

There may, of course be many more devices than have been exemplified here, depending on the installation. New devices can be created, as the hardware allows, or as needed by software expecting an I/O device with a particular alias.

## /etc

The directory */etc* is used to contain some commands which are used for maintenance of the system, and also some data files essential to the system, such as the users' password file (passwd), the mounted file table (mtab) and the message of the day (motd). A typical listing of */etc* might be:

```
$ls -l /etc
        accton      backup      checklist     cron
        dateset     ddate       dmesg         eml_tables
        ftp         getty       group         help
        init        ipldate     mkfs          mknod
        mode        motd        mount         mtab
        nunet       oldrc       passwd        pc_errors
        pcfo        pcws        pc_rterrors   rc
        squeak      ttys        uac           umount
        update      utmp
```

Many of the files in /etc are accessible only to the super-user (see Chapter 7), though some are available to all. For example, *accton* is a system accounting command. *cron* is the clock daemon which executes commands at times which have been specified by the programmer. *getty* is a process which finds the characteristics of a remote terminal at dial-up time, and tries to match the system to it. *group* is a file containing details of each user group's details.

As may be seen, /etc is a mixed bag of rarely used commands, commands which may be used only by the system supervisor, special files and daemons – self-actualising processes dealing with the 'autonomic' aspects of the system's functioning.

## /lib

The directory /lib contains a selection of library material, suited to the requirements of the users of the particular installation. It may hold assemblers, system calls and other routines which are of particular use to individuals, but it is difficult to exemplify the contents of /lib because these will vary so much from one site to another depending on the needs of the users there.

## /usr and /user

Two of the most important of the directories in / are /usr and /user. It is worth pointing out at this point a historical confusion over the naming of the directories which hold information relating to users. In Version 7 UNIX, and subsequent versions, the directory /user was used to hold users' login directories. In Version 6, and in many UNIX lookalike systems these are held in a directory within /usr. UNIX separates out into /user and /usr different aspects of user-related information.

First let's have a look at some of the contents of /user:

```
$ cd /user
$ ls -l
total 62
drwxr-xr-x 3 cl42        80 Jul 23 18:25 cl42
drwxr-xr-x 6 cla9       224 Dec 16 10:57 cla9
drwxr-xr-x 2 clb3        32 Jan  5 12:02 clb3
drwxr-xr-x 2 clb7        96 Aug  5 15:43 clb7
drwxr-xr-x 6 clj4       576 Nov  3 16:59 clj4
drwxr-xr-x 2 clj6       128 Nov 10 10:13 clj6
drwxr-xr-x 2 csj4        32 Oct 19 10:18 csj4
drwxr-xr-x 2 csj9       272 Nov 24 10:10 csj9
```

This is a list of the users of the system together with the permissions attached to their login (home) directories.

Now let's have a look at the listing of *usr* .

```
$ cd /usr
$ ls -l
total 60
drwxr-xr-x 2 root          96 Dec  6 09:49 adm
drwxr-xr-x 2 bin         1616 Jan  4 11:07 bin
drwxr-xr-x 3 bin          400 Dec 14 1981 cross
drwxr-xr-x 2 bin          128 Jul 26 1980 dict
drwxr-xr-x 2 bin           48 Nov  4 1980 doc
drwxr-xr-x 2 bin          448 Jul 26 1980 games
drwxr-xr-x 3 bin          512 Jan 20 1982 include
drwxr-xr-x12 bin          976 Jan  4 11:05 lib
drwxr-xr-x 2 root          32 Jul 26 1980 man
drwxr-xr-x 5 bin          224 Sep  9 1981 src
drwxr-xr-x 2 sys          112 Nov 12 1981 sys
```

In this particular example there are 12 directories in */usr*. The first, *adm*, contains administrative messages.

The directory *cross* relates to some cross-compilation tools for microcomputers.

The next, *dict*, is where word dictionaries for utilities such as *spell* are held.

The next one, *doc*, holds some system documentation, as does *man*, which contains the UNIX programmmer's manual, sections of which can be printed out by means of the command *man.*

The *games* directory is of course the gateway to the forbidden land of light entertainment. The last directory on the listing, *tmp*, is a repository for temporary files.

### /usr/lib and /usr/bin

Now to some of the more important directories. *Include* holds 'include' files which are frequently incorporated in programs, such as I/O routines and mathematical and special functions.

The directory *lib* contains further library files not found in */lib* itself, relating to individual users and their appplications. Similarly *bin* holds commands not found in */bin*. Here is a listing of */usr/bin*:

```
$ cd /usr/bin
$ ls
```

| | | | |
|---|---|---|---|
| arcv | awk | bas | bc |
| cal | calendar | cb | col |
| crypt | cu | date | dc |
| deroff | ed | eml | enroll |
| eqn | f77 | factor | graph |
| join | learn | lex | lint |
| look | m4 | mesg | nroff |
| plot | prep | primes | prof |
| ptx | ratfor | refer | restor |
| rev | roff | spline | split |
| struct | sum | tar | tbl |
| tc | tk | tp | tr |
| troff | tsort | uniq | units |
| uucp | uulog | uux | xget |
| xsend | yacc | | |

Many of these commands are less frequently used than those in */bin*, and in most UNIX installations the users will have set up their own command utilities in addition to those listed above, and may have discarded many of those I have listed. Nevertheless, the above does give some flavour of the contents of a typical */usr/bin* directory.

This brings us to the end of our look at the UNIX file system. There are likely to be many variations between different UNIX installations as to the details of what files are stored and where they are kept. But the information about the file system implementation itself is of universal appplicability, and the examples just given of a 'typical' file system are likely to be found true in many different places, and hopefully will prove useful as a guide to such systems in general.

# 4 Pipes and Forks

So far we have looked at the use of UNIX as a conventional operating system – one which provides utilities for handling files, devices and commands relating to them. We now turn to a consideration of features peculiar to structured operating systems of the UNIX family; particularly those relating to the use of the shell and its language.

## 4.1 The Shell

The shell is a program whose function is to interpret commands given by the user, either directly by input from a terminal or indirectly from a file. It awaits commands which come to it either from a terminal, as typed in by a user, or from a command file. When you login to the UNIX system, the shell program is running, ready to interpret commands which you may give to the system.

The UNIX system is set up to run the shell for users logging in, but it could equally well run other programs. The shell is simply the program which is left running after the system has finished bootstrapping itself.

In operating system terminology, the shell is a command decoder. While the shell is not strictly part of the operating system itself, it is through the shell that the user will usually gain access to the operating system and the facilities which it provides.

The commands in UNIX are implemented as either programs written in C (see Chapter 5) or as shell scripts – executable files using the shell (see p. 64, section 4.3).

## Commands

Let us begin with a consideration of the business of interpreting commands and what it entails. Formally, commands are defined as *words* (strings of characters) separated by blanks.

The first word is the name of the command itself. For example, in the command

```
cmp -l filea fileb
```

the word 'cmp' is taken as the name of the command. When the shell reads a command name it attempts to begin the process of carrying out that command by executing a file which has that name. (This is what carrying out a command means to the system.)

## System calls

Many commands in UNIX are implemented in terms of primitives called system calls. These are the system's building blocks which can be used for many purposes – opening and closing files, input and output, detecting signals from processes, forking, setting up pipes and others. To use these the programmer must understand the C language in depth.

## Search path

Where the shell looks for a file with the given command name depends on the search path specified by the user (more on this in section 4.8).

Usually, the search for a file with the command name is begun in the current directory, since it is quite legitimate for the user to use his own executable files as commands. If the shell fails to find the command name in the current directory it may next look in the directory /bin, since this is where the majority of standard commands are. If this fails, the search may be extended to the directory /usr/bin, where other less frequently used commands are kept. The search will be carried out in all directories specified in the user's PATH variable until the required executable file is either found or the message '<filename> not found' is output.

Having hopefully found the executable file, the shell then turns to the rest of the command. This consists of further strings, or 'words', following the command name. From the point of view of the shell, these are of three types: simple strings, strings beginning with the characters '<', '>' or '>>', and strings which contain the file expansion characters '*' and '?'.

Simple strings are understood as command arguments or as file-names, and are passed direct to the command. They modify its operation in some way.

## Special characters in commands

Strings containing special characters are scrutinised further by the shell. Those beginning with '<' or '>' are interpreted as involving redirection of the standard input or output files. The symbol '<' means that the input is to be taken from the following filename, and the symbol '>' means that output is to be sent to the following filename. Files with the appropriate names are therefore opened or created by the shell on encountering these symbols.

Strings which contain file expansion characters are taken as being the names of files which contain the characters of the string, with any other character in place of a '?' character and any other field (the string of characters before or after the period in the filename) in place of a '★' character. For example, the filename

```
text?.txt
```

would match any of the following:

```
texta.txt
textb.txt
textz.txt
text1.txt
```

The filename

```
texta.*
```

would match either:

```
texta.txt
```

or

```
texta.bak
```

Filenames are generated by the shell for any files in the current directory which fulfil these criteria. The appropriate filenames are then passed to the command in the form of an array of string data.

## Forking

Having interpreted the command line, the shell then performs a **fork**. **Fork** is a system call, and its function is to create a copy of the current process, that is, the shell itself. There are now two copies of the shell: the original one which caused the fork, and the new one.

The new shell now attempts to carry out an **execute**, which is a system call which runs the command file with the arguments passed to it. Meanwhile, the old shell waits for the new one to terminate. When it does (and the command is presumably carried out) the (old) shell goes back to its function of awaiting further input.

# Processes

It is quite important at this stage to understand what is meant by a *process*, since understanding of much of what follows depends upon this concept.

A process is an executable image of a computer's processor. This means that a process contains the state of the computer's memory, its processor flags, its input and output devices and their current state, including the files currently open.

As far as the user is concerned, processes may go on simultaneously or successively, swapping memory as required. In the example just given, the shell was the program running when the fork occurred, splitting the current state of the processor into two independently running processes. One process (the old shell) continued to function in the background, waiting for the new process (the command) to finish execution. In this case only one of the processes formed by the fork was active, while the other one waited. However more than one process can continue to run at the same time, as we shall see.

## 4.2   Pipes

Processes may communicate with one another by means of files which serve to connect the output from one process to the input of another. In the notation of the UNIX command language this is specified by a vertical bar '|' between commands calling for the processes to be connected. For example,

```
$ userprog | sort
```

will take the output of the user program *userprog*, and pass it to the system command *sort* which sorts the output in ASCII sequence. Such a link between two processes is called a *pipe*.

Pipes are a useful way of sending the output from one command or program to the input of another by means of one command line of input. There may be several steps in a line like this, setting up pipes between the parts of the line. For instance, the line:

```
$ userprog | sort | uniq
```

will take the output from the user's program, sort it and find duplicate lines anywhere in the output.

The implementation of pipes should now be fairly obvious. The execution of the first command causes a fork, the shell awaiting the termination of the command process. The presence of the 'pipe' symbol between this command and the next causes a system call **pipe**.

**Pipe** sets up files to allow the output of the first command to be directed to the input of the second. The second command brings about another fork, creating a process for the second command. The two commands now have separate processes, which communicate via the shared file, or pipe. In the meantime the shell is waiting for the processes created by it to finish. When they do, the pipe ceases to exist, along with the processes which used it.

## Pipelines

A multi-stage pipe (or **pipeline**) requires the co-existence of several processes, implemented in the way just described.

Pipes may only function in a linear way: each pipe must have two ends, and there is no way presently implemented in UNIX of getting any command to communicate directly with more than two others. This is partly because of the confusions which such communication might give rise to, such as the problems arising when inputs and outputs become 'circular', and partly because to invent and implement an acceptable general notation would be difficult.

## Redirection

Another useful consequence of the pipe implementation in UNIX is the ability to redirect input and output. We have seen that output is easily sent to a file rather than to the terminal. For instance, we could store the number of users of the system in a file called 'users' by the pipe:

```
$ ac -p | wc -l >users
```

Or we could print the number by redirecting the output of the pipe to the device which represents the printer:

```
$ ac -p | wc -l >/dev/printer
```

## Apppending to a file

The symbol '>>' causes the output to be added ('appended') to the destination instead of being written into it. Thus,

```
$ who | wc -l >>users
```

will add the number of users currently signed on to the system to the end of the file *users*, while

```
$ who | wc -l >users
```

will overwrite the previous contents of *users* (if any).

The use of the redirection facility is not limited only to output. Inputs can also be taken from sources other than the terminal. For example if we have done the pipe:

```
$ ac -p | username
```

we can subsequently do

```
$ sort <username
```

to produce an alphabetical listing of the users of the system.

Redirection is so easy in UNIX that the terminal may be thought of as just another file: the file that the system uses by default when no other has been specified.

The terminal is often taken to be the 'standard input' or 'standard output', and will be assumed to be the source of input or the destination of the output of many commands. However, there is no necessary reason why this should be so. For instance the *ed* command will expect lines from the terminal telling it how to edit a file, but if you specify that the edit commands are to be found in another file, by:

```
$ ed file <edfile
```

the command will accept this just as well.

You can use redirection of both input and output in the same command, e.g.

```
$ wc -l <username >user
```

A useful facility sometimes is the *tee* command. This enables you to copy a stream of input or output to a file and to send it to a further command at the same time. Writing

```
$ tee filename
```

causes the standard input to be sent to the standard output and also a copy of it to be written to 'filename'. If the flag -a is used, the output will be appended to the file, rather than overwriting its contents.

The pipeline

```
$ tee -a file | sh -i | tee -a file
```

should cause a copy of a terminal session to be made to 'file'.

## 4.3 Shell Scripts

The shell is a command (it is a program, and so it can be used as a command). The shell can therefore be called, and can indeed call itself. If you have a file which contains commands, the shell can be made to execute them. Typing

```
$ commandfile
```

will cause a (forked) shell program to run, and to execute the commands in *commandfile*. This is another way in which the shell can execute commands, as an aletrnative to taking its input from the keyboard of a terminal.

When the command file has been executed, control will return to the original shell, and the version of the shell process running the command file terminates. Using the shell sequences of commands can be written and executed without calling any specific programming language. Such 'shell programming' is a very powerful feature of UNIX.

## 4.4 Filters

A program which takes information from some input and passes it to an output, transforming it in some way in the process, is known as a *filter*.

An example of a filter is the *sort* program, which sorts files into ASCII character sequence. Another example would be the *prep* command which prepares a file for statistical processing by assigning one word to each line.

An example of a very powerful filter is *ed*, the text editing program. Other examples are the stream editor *sed*, and the input parser program *yacc*, and there are plenty more.

It is easy to implement the use of filters in UNIX, and the discussion of pipelines shows us one way in which filters can be easily invoked. In the following example:

```
$ ac -p | wc -l
  37
```

the command *wc* acts as a filter, counting the number of lines in the output of *ac* and thus giving us the number of users of the system. Again, in the next example the command *prep* is used to allow the words of the file *file2* to be sorted by ascending ASCII sequence.

```
$ cd john
$ prep file2 | sort
```

```
first
fourth
is
is
is
is
is
last
line
line
line
line
line
second
the
the
the
the
the
third
this
this
this
this
this
```

The facilities offered by UNIX for the use of filters are not limited to pipelines, however. The ability of the shell to process command files allows you to write programs in the command language of UNIX and have them carried out by the shell. This gives rise to the concept of 'shell programming', which is indeed programming, carried out in a very high-level language – the command language itself.

To take a simple example, suppose you want to print out the date and time every so often, as a reminder. The following shell program will do it for you:

```
while true
        do
        date
        sleep 10
        done
```

What this program does is to test the logical value of 'true', and while it is true the program carries out the loop of commands between 'do' and 'done'. In fact, the value of 'true' is always true, and so the loop goes on endlessly or until interrupted. How can we create and run this simple program?

First, the file containing the commands must be created by means of the editor, and given a name. Let's suppose that we have done this and that we have called it 'time.sh'. Inspection of the file will show that it can be read or written to, but not executed.

```
$ ls -l time.sh
-rw-rw-r-- 1 bsu6        37 Apr 19 20:13 time.sh
```

The next thing to do is therefore to make it into an executable file, by means of the *chmod* command:

```
$ chmod +x time.sh
$ ls -l time.sh
-rwxrwxr-x 1 bsu6        37 Apr 19 20:13 time.sh
```

We can now run the shell program by simply giving the command 'time.sh':

```
$ time.sh
Mon Apr 19 20:17:46 GMT 1987
Mon Apr 19 20:17:58 GMT 1987
Mon Apr 19 20:18:10 GMT 1987
Mon Apr 19 20:18:22 GMT 1987
```

and the program prints out the time every ten seconds or so, until halted.

We saw that the file 'time.sh' could be run by changing its mode so that it became executable. Such a file is known as a command file. Not all executable files contain shell commands, however. For example, a file which contains a compiled C program is executable, and can be executed from the terminal by simply typing its name. In our case we made a file of shell commands into an executable file in order to run the program of shell commands it contained. But we could have achieved the same goal in another way. Rather than changing the mode of 'time.sh' we could have left it as it was after being edited, and run it with the 'shell' command *sh*:

```
$ sh time.sh
```

The subsequent running of the program would have been the same as before.

What the *sh* command does is to execute commands read from the terminal or from a file. If the file happens to contain commands then this is equivalent to making the file executable and using it as a command itself.

The *sh* command does more than this, in fact. It is a programming language, consisting of a set of commands which can be used to build up very powerful programs using the UNIX system facilities. Let's have a look at the facilities which *sh* offers.

## 4.5  Flow Control

The shell, as we have said, is itself a programming language. Besides executing commands in UNIX or command files which have been created by the user, the shell has built into it a number of programming facilities which make the construction of shell programs easier (shell programs are sometimes referred to as shell *scripts*).

One of the most important of these facilities is the provision for writing loops and controlling program flow. We saw in the example above how a loop can be written using a *while...do* statement. The general form of the *while* is:

```
while   list1
do   list2
done
```

This command executes the first list and tests its value. The value of a list can be true (value is zero) or false (value is non-zero).

If the value of the list is zero (true) then the statement executes the second list and then tests the first list again, and so on. The loop terminates when the value of *list1* becomes non-zero (false).

An alternative form to the *while...do* statement is the *until...do*:

```
until   list1
do   list2
done
```

This statement simply reverses the sense of the test on *list1*. That is, *list2* is executed if the value of *list1* is non-zero, and the loop terminates when it is zero.

In the example on p.65 the first list consisted of the single statement 'true', which always takes the value zero (there is also a statement 'false' which is always non-zero.) The list was therefore executed indefinitely. However *list1* can be more elaborate than this.

In general, a list is any series of statements. The *value* of a list depends on the commands in it, and is usually equal to the value of the last command in the list. Commands which succeed have a value of zero. Commands which fail have non-zero values.

(The exact value taken by failed commands is an indication of the reason for their failure, and is known as a 'signal': for example, value 1 indicates an interrupt, signal value 13 indicates a write to a pipe which doesn't connect to anything.)

A control statement can therefore be made conditional upon the successful termination of a command-list or a single command, by testing the appropriate value.

Many of the commands available in the shell for flow control parallel those found in programming languages, except that in the case of shell programming you are dealing with commands instead of statements. Another form of flow control command is the *for* statement. This is similar to the *while* statement and they can sometimes be interchanged. Its general form is:

```
for  name  [in  word1 word2... ]
do  list
done
```

The *for* statement sets *name* to the first word in the word-list and executes the do-list. It then sets the name to the next word and executes the list again, and so on until the word-list is finished.

Another form of flow control command which is very useful and which again parallels the statements found in programming languages is the *if* command:

```
if  list1
then  list2
else  list3
fi
```

This is a conditional branch to one of two lists depending on the value of *list1*. If *list1* is true then *list2* is executed, otherwise *list3* is obeyed. For example, in the following shell program one of two files is listed depending on the value of the 'grep' command:

```
if grep -s . <textfile02
then
cat textfile02
else
cat textfile01
fi
```

The form of the 'grep' command (flag '-s') used here yields its status only; that is, whether file *textfile02* contains the character '.' or not. Depending on this, either *textfile01* or *textfile02* is printed. The construction 'fi' terminates the 'if' command.

The full form of the *if* command is:

```
if  list1
then  list2
elif  list3
then  list4
  .

  .
else  listn
fi
```

This form provides for long chains of tests on the exit statuses of the lists of commands. The 'elif' construction is short for 'else if'. If *list1* is not true then *list3* is evaluated, and so on for as long as required.

The final form of flow control command in the shell which we will consider is the *case* statement. Again, this parallels the familiar form in many programming languages.

The *case* statement takes the form

```
case   word   in
pattern1)   list1 ;;
pattern2)   list2 ;;
   .
   .
esac
```

The *case* command matches *word* to the patterns in turn, and executes the list associated with the first match it finds or until the *esac* is reached, for example:

```
case $1 in
a) cat filea;;
b) cat fileb;;
*) cat filec;;
esac
```

will list one of three files. If we put this text into a file called 'list', and make it executable, we can say:

```
list a
```

to list 'filea', or:

```
list b
```

to list 'fileb'. Anything else following 'list' will result in a listing of 'filec', since '*' is the default symbol meaning 'any other string.'

## 4.6 Substitutable Parameters

The *name* which was set in the *for* statement in the above example can subsequently be used in commands within the shell program. One way of doing this is to use it in a substitutable parameter. For example, in the following shell script:

```
for n in texta textb textc
do
cat $n
done
```

the name 'n' is set, in turn, to 'texta', 'textb' and 'textc'. These three files are then listed on the terminal. The '$' symbol introduces a *substitutable parameter;* in this case the name 'n'. The parameter takes the values which have been assigned to it elsewhere. Parameters can be used inside or outside the shell script. For example we could say:

```
cat $n
```

and put this into a shell script called 'list'. If we now make 'list' an executable file by means of *chmod* we can give the command:

```
list filex
```

to obtain a listing of *filex*. This is of course trivial, but shows the ability to substitute names for parameters in shell scripts.

The shell provides a further list of parameters which are identified by their position in the range of integers from 1 to n. These are known by the names $1, $2, etc, and can be set and used in shell scripts. Positional parameters can be set by the shell *set* command. In the following example, the output is the same as that of the previous one:

```
set texta textb textc
cat $1
cat $2
cat $3
```

Once again, we can have the script:

```
cat $1
cat $2
cat $3
```

and put it in an executable file called 'list'. Issuing the command:

```
list filea fileb filec
```

has the effect of substituting the arguments following 'list' for the parameters $1, $2 and $3 in sequence.

If you have a lot of parameters to deal with it may be convenient to use the *shift* command. This puts the value of parameter $2 into $1, $3 into $2 and so on, leaving $n vacant. In the next example the output is as before:

```
set texta textb textc
for i in 1 2 3
do
cat $1
shift
done
```

In the case of a large number of parameters this can be easier to deal with.

In addition to the flow control commands discussed previously, there is also a command called *test*. This enables the shell programmer to test the status of files. It takes the form:

```
test [flags] filename
```

Flags in *test* can take values allowing testing for the type of file, for example whether it is a directory, the status of files, e.g. whether they are writable or readable, and for a number of other conditions.

For example, if the flag '-f' is used, the *test* command returns 'true' exit status if the file exists, 'false' if it does not exist. In the following example, the flag '-d' is used to test whether the file is a directory: if it is the command returns 'true':

```
if test -d $1
echo 'cannot cat directory'
else
cat $1
fi
```

If this is put into an executable file it will type out non-directory files using *cat* but will print out an error message if you try to type a directory.

## 4.7 String Variables

Besides the substitutable parameters, the shell provdes for string variables, which can be known by name and set by the user. For example:

```
fred=john
```

or

```
fred=/user/richard/john
```

set the value of 'fred' to the string following the '='. The string variable can then be used in substitutable form with a preceding '$' in the shell script. For example, the following script:

```
h=/user/richard
echo $h
```

if put into the executable file 'home' will print out the pathname of the home directory whenever the command

```
$ home
```

is given.

71

One useful feature of shell programming is the facility of writing input to a shell procedure within the shell script itself. This can be done by sandwiching the input (called a 'here' document) between the symbols '<<string' and 'string'. For example, the following script, where 'string' = '%', will list the 'here' document itself:

```
cat <<%
This is line one
This is line two
This is line three%
```

Another example might be input to an edit command, which can be easily specified within the shell procedure doing the editing. For instance the procedure

```
ed $1 <<%
1,$s/bsu6/richard/%
```

if put into the executable file 'edit' will make all references to 'bsu6' in 'afile' into 'richard' when the command:

```
edit afile
```

is given.

## 4.8 The Environment

The shell runs in the context of a series of special parameters which are passed to each program that it executes. For example, the parameter TERM specifies the type of terminal, as in the command

```
TERM=vt100
```

These parameters constitute the environment of the shell, and are used by it in various ways.

Parameters of the environemnt which are required by the shell include: HOME, which gives the home directory; PATH which specifies the directories to be searched by the shell for executable commands; MAIL, the value of the mailbox; and the prompt strings PS1 and PS2, used by the shell to prompt for commands.

These parameters are usually set up at the time of login by means of a file called .profile. A file of this name is automatically looked for by the shell, and then executed. An example of a .profile file might be:

```
$ ed .profile
?.profile
a
TERM=vt100
PATH=.:/bin:/usr/bin:/usr/local/bin:/usr/lib:
```

```
/usr/ucb:/etc PS1="rc> "
export PATH TERM
.
w
88
q
```

The values of any parameters set in the environment can be examined by means of the *set* command

```
set
HOME=/user/friends/bsu6
IFS='
'
PATH=.:/bin:/usr/bin:/usr/local/bin:/usr/lib:
/usr/ucb:/etc
PS1='rc '
PS2=' '
SHELL=/bin/sh
TERM=vt100
USER=richard
```

## Exporting parameters

The use of the *export* command in the above example is important. Communication between a shell procedure and the shell calling it may be set up by means of the parameters passed between them. Just as a program calling a subroutine can pass parameters to it, so the shell can pass parameters to a shell program. This is done by means of the *export* command:

```
export name
```

This tells the shell that the variable *name* can be used in a shell program. When a variable is exported, a copy of it is made for use by the shell program, so that the original is not altered inadvertently. (This corresponds to the 'call by value' of subroutine implementation.)

To make absolutely sure that no alteration is made to a variable, the statement *readonly* may be used:

```
readonly name
```

ensures that the value of *name* cannot change in the procedure.

The shell can read input by means of the *read* command, which assigns input words to specified variables in the same order as they occur in the input line:

```
read name1 name2 ....
```

In the following example, the *read* command is used to acquire a dialogue with a UNIX system by writing the user's messages to the system and the system's replies to a single file:

```
read a
while test -n $a
do
echo $a >temp
cat temp >>perm
chmod +x temp
temp >temp1
cat temp1
cat temp1 >>perm
read a
done
```

## 4.9  Executable Files

As mentioned earlier in this chapter, a shell script can only be executed if it is in a file which can itself be executed. We have seen one way of doing this: the file is made executable by changing the permission bit and is then executed by giving its name.

Another way of executing a shell program is to use the sh command. This will execute the file without changing its permission bits. Thus:

```
$ sh file
```

is functionally equivalent to

```
$ chmod u+x file
$ file
```

although *sh* leaves the permission bits unchanged.

## 4.10  Alternative Shells

It will be noticed that the shell to be run is shown by the set command. The shell run in the examples used is */bin/sh*. Alternative shells could be set up to be run by means of the user's profile. As mentioned above, the shell is simply the program which is usually run on logging in, because it provides the facilities most users require.

There are a number of different shell programs available. Differences in the shell will provide different facilities. The shell most often used is the **Bourne shell**, and that is the one discussed here.

The shell is very powerful. Jobs which would otherwise require long and tedious assembly language programming can be carried out by a shell procedure: simpler jobs may be done by a one-line command pipeline. The shell has sufficient contact with computer hardware to enable it to control things at the level of input and output, but at the same time gives high-level facilities for writing procedures. It can be seen that the shell offers almost unlimited programming possibilities.

# 5 The C Programming Language

## 5.1 The Importance of C to UNIX

The implementation of UNIX has for some years been carried out in a programming language called C. Appropriately enough, C is the successor to a language called B, both of which were in turn based on another language; BCPL. C is generally thought of as a low-level language despite its structured nature, since it retains the ability to deal with hardware in a similar way to assembly languages.

As well as being used to implement UNIX, C has been the medium in which much UNIX-related software has been written, and it has also been adopted by the writers of other structured operating systems of the UNIX family.

### Portability

C has two other features which have ensured its success, even without its associations with UNIX. It is highly *portable*, that is, programs written in C can be moved from one hardware environment to another, or from one operating system to another, with minimal difficulty. The advantages of this in terms of economy of effort, when new machines replace old ones, need no clarification.

C is also a highly structured language; it has, as we shall see, the characterstics needed to encourage good programming.

As a result of these features C has attained a great deal of popularity, and compilers now exist for most major mainframes and minicomputers, and for an increasing number of microcomputers also. As well as being written in C, UNIX offers the language as a facility to the users of the system.

UNIX is often transported from one machine to another or from one software environment to another by means of C. UNIX systems are highly portable, and this portability is achieved because the UNIX system is written in the C language. In order to transport UNIX to another environment it is not necessary to rewrite the whole system:

instead, if there is a C compiler for the target system, UNIX can be assembled to run on it. Even if there is no C compiler already in existence on the target system, it is probably much easier to write one than to rewrite UNIX in the native language of the target system.

## 5.2 Characteristics of C

It can be appreciated that for these reasons, a grasp of C is of considerable importance to the user who wants to fully exploit the potential of his system. We will look first of all at the broad characteristics of the language.

### Block structure

C has a well-defined block structure, in which statements are grouped together, and in which any statement can be itself replaced by a block of statements. This encourages a well-disciplined approach to the writing of programs. In particular it means that the temptation to write *goto* statements is lessened, and it is easier to avoid writing what is sometimes called 'spaghetti' code.

Control of flow in a block-structured language tends to be achieved by means of *for, do-while* and *if-else* constructions, which keep the destination within the block. It is possible to *goto* addresses outside the block, but it is argued that the likelihood of a programming error being made in this way is reduced in a language which provides a block structure.

### Typing

Unlike BCPL and B, which are 'typeless' languages, C uses a wide variety of data type declarations. Some of these are of the kind familiar to users of languages such as Algol, Fortran and PL/1: and provide arrays, integer and floating-point variables and character formats. Other data types may be made up out of simpler types used in combination. Variables of mixed types may also be held together in the same structure, in the same kind of way as they are in Cobol.

### Mixed types

It may be desirable for a particular machine to interpret the same data as being of several different types. In C, a structure called a *union* will hold data of alternative types at different times. This is an important feature of a language which requires the programmer to specify the type of data he is using. Declarations may be made at different levels, depending on the lifetime which they are required to have: for example, declarations made inside a function or subprogram exist only in that subprogram.

## 5.3 Structure of a C Program

Formally, a C program consists of a series of *declarations*, which may be of two kinds: declarations of functions, and data declarations. The program statements occur inside functions. The whole of a C program is itself a function, called *main*, and within it the other function calls are embedded. A function has the following form:

```
function name (arguments)
argument declarations
{
declarations
statements
}
```

### Arguments

Various parts of this structure may be absent. For example, there may be no arguments within the parentheses '( )' (and hence no argument declarations), or there may be no declarations inside the braces'{ }', which are like the *begin* and *end* of Algol, or the DO (statement number) of Fortran. There need not even be any statements in the body of the function. The spacing of the parts of the function on different lines is to some extent arbitrary, and is done to make the structure clearer. A function which does nothing would look like this:

```
null() {}
```

This shows the bare bones of the function only.
   A very short C program looks like this:

```
main()
{
        printf("hello!\n");
}
```

This program prints the word 'hello!' on a line by itself. Although it is in itself trivial, it is worth seeing how to go through the process of writing, compiling and running it, since this is how all C programs can be prepared and run from a terminal.

The program consists, first, of a 'main' function with no parameters. The body of the function follows, with one statement inside the braces. This statement is another function, this time one called 'printf', and it is terminated with a semi-colon ';'. The function 'printf' prints its own arguments, which are placed in double quotes. The construction '\n' which appears within the quotes means 'newline' and will result in a new line following the printing of the word 'hello!'.

## 5.4  Writing C Programs

To write this program you must first invoke the editor and enter the lines of the C program:

```
$ ed
a
main()
{
?printf("hello!\n");
}
.
```

The character '?' in the line containing the *printf* function is a tab character, as we can see when the buffer is listed:

```
1,$p
main()
{
        printf("hello!\n");
}
```

## Source files

This now looks like the example above, so we can write it to a file. Source files for C programs must have a '.c' suffix. Let us call the source file for this program 'hello.c'

```
w hello.c
31
q
```

## Compiling C programs

Having quit the editor we can now compile the program with the *cc* command:

```
$ cc hello.c
```

If we have not made any mistakes, such as putting the wrong sort of brackets in a particular place, the program should compile, giving no messages (usually a good sign in UNIX).

The compiled program in an executable form will be put into a default file called 'a.out'. It can be run simply by giving this name as a command to the shell:

```
$ a.out
hello!
```

This last line is the output from your program. Although rather insignificant looking in itself, if you have actually written, compiled and run this example the reward will be out of proportion to the size of the output!

Let us try another example, this time a program with two statements, which will say 'hello and goodbye!':

```
$ ed
a
main()
{
?printf("hello ");
?printf("and goodbye!"\n");
}
.
1,$p
main()
        printf("hello ");
        printf("and goodbye!\n"); ;
}
w avesal.c
57
q
$ cc avesal.c
$ a.out
hello and goodbye!
```

## Escape sequences

One or two points should now be made clear concerning program writing in general. The above example program contains no declarations, since it does not use any variables. The string of characters in quotes is printed out exactly as it appears in the program up to the '\', and is called a string constant. The '\' heralds the start of an 'escape sequence' which is a series of characters which are unlikely to be found anywhere else in the program and which perform a special function, in this case printing a newline. Other escape sequences are:

'\t'   which prints a tab character,
'\b'   which is a backspace,
'\"'   which prints a double quote, and
'\\'   for printing the backslash itself.

Here is how to enter and run a program which prints out the escape sequences for these four special characters:

```
$ ed
a
main()
{
?printf("tab is \\t\n");
?printf("backspace is \\b\n");
?printf("quote is \\"\n");
?printf("backslash is \\\\\n");
}
.
1,$p
main()
{
        printf("tab is \\t\n");
        printf("backspace is{ \\b\n");
        printf("quote is \\\"\n");
        printf("backslash is \\\\\n");
}
w    four.c
128
q
$ cc four.c
$ a.out
tab is \t
backspace is \b
quote is \"
backslash is \\
```

As will already have become apparent, statements are terminated by a semicolon ';'. Statements can be grouped together with the braces '{}' (as they are in a function) for other purposes also, such as looping in the body of a *for* statement. Here is an example of a program which uses a *for* loop to iterate the conversion of temperature measurements from Centigrade to Fahrenheit:

```
$ ed convert.c
a
/* Program to convert Fahrenheit to Centigrade */
main()
{
        float cent,fahr;
        for (fahr=0; fahr<=120; fahr = fahr + 10)
        {
                cent = (fahr-32.0)*(5.0/9.0);
                printf("%6.1f %6.1f\n", fahr, cent);
        }
}
.
w
215
q
$ cc convert.c
$ a.out
     0  -17.8
    10  -12.2
    20   -6.7
    30   -1.1
    40    4.4
    50   10.0
    60   15.6
    70   21.1
    80   26.7
    90   32.2
   100   37.8
   110   43.3
   120   48.9
```

## Comments

There are many similarities with other languages. Comments in a C program are enclosed between '/*' and '*/'. Output is formatted, as in the above the '%6.1f' format means 'print a floating-point number with a field-width of 6, with one decimal place.'

## Declarations

Notice the declaration 'float', for the variables 'cent' and 'fahr'. This means that they are single-precision floating-point quantities.

# Loops

The above example uses a *for* loop. Another useful way of writing loops in C is to use the *while* construction. See how the previous example would look if it were rewritten to use a *while* statement instead of a *for* statement:

```
/* Program to convert Fahrenheit to Centigrade */
main()
{
        float cent, fahr;
        fahr = 0.0;
        while (fahr <= 120.0)
        {
                cent = (fahr-32.0)*(5.0/9.0);
                printf("%6.1f %6.1f\n", fahr, cent);
                fahr = fahr+10.0;
        }
} .
```

The contents of the braces following the *while* statement are executed repeatedly until the *condition* in brackets just after the word 'while' no longer applies. A *while* statement can be made to perform a single statement only or, as it was here, a block of statements enclosed in braces.

The difference between the two forms of loop instruction is a slight one, and one form can usually be converted into the other without much bother. However, usually one or the other is more convenient in a particular context. In this case, the *for* statement is probably better, because it does the incrementing of 'fahr' as part of the initialisation of the loop. The *while* statement necessitates doing the incrementing as part of the body of the loop. You also have to initialise 'fahr' in a separate statement. However there is probably not a lot in it in this instance. Where complex logical conditions are involved the *while* is undoubtedly both easier to use and clearer to read.

## 5.5 Programming Style

C is a language which assists the programmer in writing programs in a good 'style' (for stimulating tutorial discussions of 'style' in its broadest sense, see Kernighan and Plauger's excellent texts *The Elements of Programming, Software Tools,* and *Software Tools in Pascal*).

For instance, it is not good programming practice to have constants embedded in a program which may need to be changed at some future time. It means that you have to go through the program looking for these 'magic numbers' and changing them, and there is always the lurking danger that one will be missed. It also makes a great deal more work than is necessary.

A much better way to handle constants which may need to be changed is to make them into *symbolic constants.* A symbolic constant is a name (like 'fahr' or 'cent') which is conventionally written in upper case characters to indicate that it stands for a constant. The value of the symbolic constant may be given at the beginning of the program or program block, by means of a *£define:* e.g

```
£define START 0.0
```

Whenever you use the symbolic constant 'START' in the program following this definition the C compiler will substitute the constant 0.0. We could thus rewrite the conversion program (the first version, using a *for* loop) in this way:

```
/* Program to convert Fahrenheit to Centigrade */
£defineSTART0.0/* Start of  for  loop */
£defineEND300.0/* End of  for  loop */
£define STEP10.0/* Step size */
main()
{
        float cent,fahr;
        for (fahr=START; fahr<=END; fahr = fahr + STEP)
        {
                cent = (fahr-32.0)*(5.0/9.0);
                printf("%6.1f %6.1f n", fahr, cent);
        }
}
```

If you then want to alter the range or step size of the conversion table, all that you need to do is to substitute a new 'define' statement for the appropriate constant symbol. Once again, in a program as short as this one to apply, it hardly seems to matter, but the principal is a sound one, and may save a lot of work.


## 5.6  Arithmetic in C

The arithmetic conventions in C are much like those in other languages. The arithmetic operators '+' and '−' have their usual meaning, and have the same priority, in a left-to-right sequence of evaluation. The same is true of '★' and '/', which take a higher priority than '+' and '−'. There is an operator '%' (not to be confused with the '%' sign used in formatting), called the *modulus operator,* which can be used in integer division to produce the remainder, e.g.:

    10 % 4

gives the result

    2

It is sometimes found confusing that C uses the same symbol, e.g. the '%' sign for two or more different purposes. This is one of the things which makes C an unpopular language with some users. There is, however, no ambiguity in context.

There is no C operator for exponentiation.

The rules of arithmetic are also fairly straightforward. As we have seen already, there are the two common data types *int* and *float,* and something of how they can be manipulated. Arithmetic conversions are performed as needed: e.g. when adding an *int* and a *float* the result will be a *float.* There are a few other data types, e.g. *double,* which specifies a double-precision floating-point number, and *char* which defines a single byte.

## 5.7  Input and Output

Now here is a program to read in characters and output them again.

```
main()      /*  Copy input to output  */
{
        int c;

        c=getchar();
        while (c != EOF)
        {
                putchar(c);
                c=getchar();
        }
}
```

## End of file

The value 'EOF' is £defined to take the value −1, so the program proceeds as long as the input character is not equal to ('!=') −1.

This program introduces the input and output functions 'getchar' and 'putchar'. Like so many progamming languages, C feels that it ought not to soil its hands with the real world, and these input and output functions are not really part of C at all, so the operating system environment provides input-output.

The operating system recognises the 'getchar' function as meaning 'Get one character from the input device (in this case, the terminal).' Similarly, 'putchar' writes a character out on the terminal.

## 5.8 More on Typing

We have used the function 'getchar( )' to return the next character (or characters) from a terminal input line. Since any character may be typed in, the function 'getchar( )' must be able to handle them. The statement:

```
c=getchar();
```

might therefore be expected to return a character to 'c', and we might also expect to see 'c' declared as a character variable. However, it is often convenient to write routines which use the numeric integer value corresponding to an input character rather than the character itself. It is better in this case if 'c' is defined as an *int* variable. It is all right to do this, since the conversion between data type 'char' and 'int' is automatically carried out by the assignment statement. By way of example, consider the following two programs:

```
main()
{
        int c;

        label:c=getchar();
        printf("%d\n", c);
        goto label
}

main()
{
        char c;

        label:c=getchar();
        printf("%c\n", c);
        goto label
}
```

Compare the output of these two programs, and see the difference brought about by the automatic conversion to 'int' which happens in arithmetic where 'char' and 'int' data types are used together.

Notice also, in passing, the use of the reprehensible 'goto' statement, which is available in C. I have used it here because otherwise an end of file problem arises: how to detect the last character. As it is, the problem has not been solved, merely shelved, since you have to exit from either program by means of some predetermined 'break' character which the system you are using recognises. The solution to this problem is to look for an end-of file indicator of some kind, say a negative value, and we shall see this used in the next example.

## Float and double

In addition to the data types already mentioned, there are others of a kind familiar from languages such as Fortran and PL/1. 'Float' is a general purpose arithmetic type declaration; for greater precision the declaration 'double' can be used, giving double precision floating-point numbers. Integers can be 'short', 'int' or 'long', the idea being that only the appropriate amount of storage space will be used. (In many machines however there is no difference between the 'int' and 'long' declarations.)

## Use of arrays

Arrays are available in C, and these can hold numbers or characters. Let's see how arrays are used, in a program to count the number of digits of different values in an input file. There are ten digit types, so an array able to hold the count for each of these must be used. The program also shows the use of conditional statements in C:

```
main()
{
            int digit[10];
            int c, i;
            for (i = 0; i < 10; ++i) digit[i]=0;
            {
                    while ((c = getchar()) >= 0)
                    {
                            if (c >= 0) if (c <= 9)
                            digit[c] = digit[c] + 1;
                            else
                            else
                    }
            }
```

```
                     printf ("digitn=\n") ;
                     for (i = 0; i <= 10; i = ++i)
                     printf ("%d %d\n", i+1, digit [i] ) ;
         }
```

The construction '++' means 'increment by 1', and is a quick way of stepping on a counter. The problem of end-of-file is solved by the construction '((c = getchar( )) >= 0)', which allows you to read a character and test its value in one line.

## 5.9  Block Structure

The 'if' statement as used in the above example takes the form:

```
if (condition)
statement
else
statement
```

As elsewhere in C, a block of statements enclosed in braces can be substituted for either of the single statements. If there is no left-hand brace following the 'condition' or 'else' then the compiler assumes that only one statement is to be executed, thus defining the limits of the 'if-true' and 'if-false' parts of the compound 'if' statement. The 'else' part of the statement can be omitted if there is no statement following it. In the above example, the two 'else' lines could, therefore, have been left out.

### Use of 'else' statement

The 'else' statement can be extended like this:

```
if (condition)
statement
else if (condition)
statement
else if (condition)
statement
      .
      .
else
statement
```

Once again, the final 'else' may be omitted if there is no statement following it.

## Switches

Another form of conditional statement is the 'switch'. In this example, a 'switch' statement is used instead of an 'if' (somewhat redundantly) to count the number of occurrences of the digits 0 to 9 in the input file.

```
main ()
{
            int c, i;
            int digit[10];

            for (i = 0; i <= 9; i++)
            digit[i] = 0;

            while ((c = getchar()) < 0)
            switch (c)
            {
                        case '0':
                        case '1':
                        case '2':
                        case '3':
                        case '4':
                        case '5':
                        case '6':
                        case '7':
                        case '8':
                        case '9':
                        digit[i]++;
                        break;
                        default:
                        break;
            }

            printf("digitn=\n");
            for (i = 0; i <= 9; i = ++i)
            printf("%d %d\n", i+1, digit[i]);
}
```

The use of 'switch' is fairly self-explanatory. Each of the 'case' options may be followed by a statement (or block). If none of the cases is met, a general 'default' option allows another statement to be executed.

In the above example each of the first ten cases requires identical treatment. Some provision has to be made to make sure that the 'switch' loop is exited after the required action has been performed for a particular case. This provision is met by means of the 'break' statement, which forces an exit from a loop. (If more than one loop is in progress, the break takes you to the next innermost loop, and not out of all the loops, as in some languages.)

## 5.10 Functions

So far, although we have used functions, such as *main* and *printf*, we have not seen in any detail how functions are written. As we saw earlier, a function has the form:

```
function name (arguments)
argument declarations
{
declarations
statements
}
```

and it was stated that some of these parts of a function may be missing. Let us see this structure realised in a function called 'fact' which is designed to calculate the factorial of an integer n. (The factorial of n, usually written n! in mathematcial notation and sometimes pronounced 'n shriek', is defined as:

```
n! = n  * (n-1) * (n-2) * . . . . . * 2 * 1
```

or, if you prefer a recursive definition:

```
n! = 1 if n = 1
n! = n * (n-1)! if n > 1)
```

### Defining a function

Here is the function:

```
fact (n)
int n;
{
        int m, f;

        f=1;
        for (m=1; m=n; ++m)
        f=m*f;
        return (f);
}
```

### Use of a function

The function 'fact' can now be used in a program such as the following:

```
main ()
{
        int x;

        printf ("Number\tFactorial\n");
        or (i = 0; i <= 10; ++i)
        printf ("%3d %8d\n", i, fact(i));
}
```

## Call by value

Functions in C have their parameters passed to them by value: that is, they get a copy of the value of the parameter and they cannot therefore change the original value inadvertantly. This contrasts with other languages which pass parameters by reference (e.g. by name) allowing access to the argument values themselves.

## Function results

The result of a function is designated by means of the 'return' statement, if there is one (functions do not need to return a result). This return value is accessed by the function call itself, which acts as the name of the value returned by the function, as in the example just given. Unfortunately, this method of treating parameters has some limitations: it is impossible for example to return the parameters used in the function call with new values, as might be required by a function:

```
swap (a,b)
```

firstly because the paramaters cannot be altered, and secondly because only one paramater can be returned anyway. Returned values can, of course, be of any legitimate data type.

## Scope

The discussion of functions raises once again the question of *scope*, that is, the extent to which a value-name can be recognised within a program. As we have seen, at least implicitly, declarations within a function apply inside the function only. If we write a function called 'character' and define an integer within it called 'c':

```
character (c)
{
int c;
```

we cannot use the name 'c' outside the function and expect it to retain its meaning. We can even use the same name inside and outside a function and be confident that it will mean two completely separate things. What can be said in general about names and where they can be validly used?

If you want a name, for instance the name of an *int* variable, to apply throughout a program, you must make it into an *external variable*. This means that it is defined outside any function which could want to use it, usually at the beginning of the program. Having been defined externally, the variable may be used in any function by declaring it as *extern*, in the function itself. The structure of the program would look like this:

```
int c;
.
.
main()
{
.
.
function1(w,x)
.
.
extern int c;
{
.
.
.
}
.
.
function2(y,z,r)
.
extern int c;
{
.
.
.
}
.
.
.
}
```

## Declaring and defining

At this point it is worth emphasising the distinction between *declaring* and *defining* a name. The declaration of a variable states its properties (e.g. size and type of variable) but it does not reserve any memory for the variable or put any value into it. The definition on the other hand causes memory to be reserved, and may also set it to a certain value. In the present context this means that an external variable must be defined before it can be used; in addition, however, it must be declared (and be available to be declared) before its actual use in a particular part of the program.

## Automatic and static variables

If a variable is not defined as external but is local to a function it is known as 'automatic'. Automatic variables lose their values outside the function in which they are defined. Nor do they retain a value between one call of the function and another. It is possible to define variables which do not change between calls in the way that automatics do, and such variables are called 'static'. Static variables can be either local or external in their scope. There is also the class of 'register' variables, a term which denotes frequent use. The compiler will put such variables into actual machine registers where possible, thus saving time in fetching them from memory.

## Structures

One last data type which is well worth detailed attention is the *structure*. In some ways a structure resembles an array, in that it can hold a number of items in a single named part of storage. However a structure can hold items of different types, e.g. integers and characters, together. For instance, a structure could be declared for a payee who is employed by a firm, and might look like this:

```
struct payee
{
            int number;
            int location;
            char name[20];
            int taxcode;
            float pay-to-date;
            float tax-to-date;
            float hours-work;
};
```

This declaration of the structure gives the 'tag' 'payee' to the template defined by the list of members of the specified data types. As with other declarations, it does not reserve memory unless there is also a *definition* of the variables. This could be done later by a statement such as:

```
struct payee p = ( 207, 26, Robinson, 403, 10500.5, .5,
3000.25, 48);
```

which would define the variable 'p' to be a structure of the sort already declared, and initialise its members to the values corresponding to their declared order. If we now want to refer to a member of the structure 'p' we can do it by a name of the form:

```
structure.member
```

For instance we could say:

```
t = p.tax;
```

to set the variable 't' to the value of the tax-code.


## Pointers

Another way of referring to the members of a structure is the *pointer*. If we declare a structure:

```
struct payee *ptr;
```

then 'ptr' becomes a *pointer* to the structure of type 'payee'. The members of the structure can thereafter be referred to by the notation:

```
ptr-> member
```

For example,

```
t = ptr->tax
```

This has necessarily been a highly abbreviated account of some of the features of the C language. In particular, there are many more data types and means of accessing data than have been mentioned here. However, this chapter may have served to give something of the flavour of C. If you try to use it you will soon discover how powerful it is and how much can be done in a very concise manner. The main advantages of C are that it is highly portable and that it provides structured programming facilities but still allows access to machine-level features.

The relationship between C and UNIX has already been mentioned. Many UNIX-like systems are implemented in C, and it is not too difficult to see how some of the UNIX commands could be implemented (if you read The *C Programming Language* by Brian W Kernighan and Dennis M Ritchie you will find many examples of this.)

Conversely, the C compiler functions under many forms of UNIX. This language is therefore not only a useful tool in programming but is also the foundation-stone of UNIX and all the other systems which have sprung from it.

Readers who wish to learn more about C will find *The Professional Programmers Guide to C,* published by Pitman in this series of books, a lucid and informative tutorial introduction to writing well-structured programs in C.

# 6 Text Handling in UNIX

In this chapter we shall examine some of the facilities for text handling in UNIX. We shall begin with the text editor *ed*, and progress to some of the more recondite commands such as *sed*, *awk* and *yacc*.

## 6.1 The Text Editor – *ed*

In order to show the facilities of *ed* in detail, let us go through the process of inputting and editing some text. I have chosen a poem called *The Private of the Buffs* by Sir Francis Hastings Doyle. First we invoke the editor:

```
$ ed poem1
?poem1
```

The editor responds to the filename with an error message ('?'), but it remembers it in case there is a subsequent write command without a filename. In this event it will write the output to the file *poem1*. We now type in the text:

```
a
Last night, among his fellow roughs,
He jested, quaffed and swore;
Adrunken private of the Buffs
Who never looked before.
Today,beneath the foe?m{aS's frown
He stands in Elgin's place:
Ambassador of Britains crown
And type of all her race.
Aye! tear his body limb from limb:
Bring cord or axe roor flame!
He only knows that not through him
Shall England come to shame.
Poor, reckless, ,orudede, lowborn, untaught,
Bewildered and alone,
A heaetrt with English instinct fraught
He yet can call his own
.
w
496
```

As you can easily see, some gremlins have got into this poem; mainly as a result of a noisy telephone line, though partly due to a combination of finger-trouble and a bad memory. However, it is not as bad as it looks, as we can see by printing out the contents of the buffer:

```
1,$p
Last night, among his fellow roughs,
He jested, quaffed and swore;
Adrunken private of the Buffs
Who never looked before.
Today,beneath the foe?m{aS's frown
He stands in Elgin's place:
Ambassador of Britains crown
And type of all her race.
Aye! tear his body limb from limb:
Bring cord or axe or flame!
He only knows that not through him
Shall England come to shame.
Poor, reckless, rudede, lowborn, untaught,
Bewildered and alone,
A heart with English instinct fraught
He yet can call his own
```

(If you want to follow the examples which follow, you should now enter the above text, just as it appears here).

## Deleting and replacing lines

The spelling of 'heart' is correct, and only appeared to be wrong because of the way the terminal had treated some delete characters when I was typing it in. The fifth line is a hopeless mess, however, and may as well be deleted and replaced, using the *d* and *a* commands. These will address specified line numbers: first we will delete line 5, and then we will insert the new line 5 after line 4:

```
5d
4a
Today, beneath the foeman's frown
```

It is worth noticing that, after having deleted line 5, we could have inserted the new line in one of two ways; either by appending it after line 4, which we did, or, equivalently, by inserting it before line 5. The formulation we used is perhaps less confusing, for the inserted line is itself to be the new line 5.

## Moving lines

There is a whole block of lines in the wrong place in this poem, because the last and last-but-one verses got put in in the wrong order. In *ed* it is easy to move a block of lines by means of the *m* command:

```
9,12m16
```

This moves lines 9 to 12 inclusive to after line 16. (Notice that the destination is specified by its position *before* the move takes place, rather than after.)

Let us now inspect the result again:

```
1,$p
Last night, among his fellow roughs,
He jested, quaffed and swore;
Adrunken private of the Buffs
Who never looked before.
Today, beneath the foeman's frown,
He stands in Elgin's place:
Ambassador of Britains crown
And type of all her race.
Poor, reckless, rudede, lowborn, untaught,
Bewildered and alone,
A heart with English instinct fraught
He yet can call his own
Aye! tear his body limb from limb:
Bring cord or axe or flame!
He only knows that not through him
Shall England come to shame.
```

## Substituting text

This begins to look better. There are still some spelling mistakes, however. 'Adrunken' is obviously wrong, and the spelling of 'rude' (for that is what it is meant to be) in line 9 needs correcting. To do this we can use the *s* command which has the form:

```
(.,.)s/expression/replacement/
```

This command searches the buffer between the line numbers specified and replaces the expression on each line where it finds it. E.g.

```
1,$s/Ad/A d/
```

This is the shortest possible string which could be used to make the correction, and in this case it is safe enough to use it, because it is unlikely that such a sequence as 'Ad' would occur elsewhere in the poem. This might not be true of some other passages of prose or even poetry, since many sentences could begin in this way. Let us now try to correct the other spelling mistake:

```
1,$s/rudede/rude./
?
```

But here something has gone wrong. The editor queries the command, indicating that for some reason it cannot be carried out. Queried commands may be incorrect in form, or there may be some other reason why a perfectly correct-looking command cannot be performed. In this case, the expression 'rudede' could not be found by the editor, and so it printed an error message. Had the expression been found, there would not have been any message printed, indicating the successful execution of the command.

It is apparent that the word is badly garbled: it prints as 'rudede' but must contain other characters which print in this way. Let us try another form of the *s* command which uses the 'wild card' character '.'. This character when placed in the search expression matches any character. The problem is that we don't know which characters are valid ones, yet in order to carry out the *s* command we must be able to match something. Let us try assuming that the first three characters are valid:

```
1,$s/rud.../rude/
```

The command has worked, since no error message was returned. Let us check again. We could do this by printing out the whole of the buffer once more, but a quicker way is simply to check the line which has been altered. After the *s* command has been carried out, a pointer is left set to the value of the last line affected by the command. This value is known as the currently addressed line, and all commands affecting the value of the current line number specify to what value it will be set after the command has been carried out. We can inspect this line by giving the *p* command with the argument '.', meaning the value of the currently addressed line, which in this case is the line we want to inspect.

```
.P
Poor, reckless, rude, lowborn, untaught,
```

Good. The text now looks like this:

```
1,$p
Last night, among his fellow roughs,
He jested, quaffed and swore;
A drunken private of the Buffs
```

```
Who never looked before.
Today, beneath the foeman's frown,
He stands in Elgin's place:
Ambassador of Britains crown
And type of all her race.
Poor, reckless, rude, lowborn, untaught,
Bewildered and alone,
A heart with English instinct fraught
He yet can call his own
Aye! tear his body limb from limb:
Bring cord or axe or flame!
He only knows that not through him
Shall England come to shame.
```

## Joining lines

Another feature of the editor is that it allows you to join two lines
together, which in this case would result in the poem having very long
lines, though they would still make sense. Let us join up the last two
lines using the *j* command:

```
15,16j
```

### Implied print command

Instead of giving the command *p* to check the line it is sufficient to
type the line number by itself to cause that line to be printed out. Since
the line we want printed is the current line we can just put:

```
.
He only knows that not through himShall England come
to shame.
```

This needs editing to get rid of the capitalisation and insert a space in
the middle of the line:

```
s/mS/m s/
.
He only knows that not through him shall England come
to shame.
```

## Undo command

In fact, it would be a tedious and rather pointless exercise to go through the poem joining the lines together in this way; so let's abandon it at this point and put the line back as it was.

If you make an alteration using the editor commands and then decide you have made a mistake, you can undo the effect of the last command by means of the *u* command, thus:

```
u
.
He only knows that not through himShall England come
to shame.
```

Unfortunately you can only undo the last edit command in this way! Let us restore the last two lines and write the edited version of the poem: *The Private of the Buffs*:

```
s/mS/m\
S/
w poem1
493
```

## Handling special characters

The last emendation to the poem was the insertion of a newline between its last two lines. If we had tried to add the newline in the obvious way it would have resulted in failure, e.g.

```
s/mS/m
?
S
?
/
?
```

The newline character is interpreted as the end of the command, and subsequent characters are errors. In order to insert a newline we can use the backslash '\', which is an escape character meaning 'literally the next character.'

The backslash can be used to manipulate a number of awkward characters, including the backslash itself; the construction:

```
/\/
```

won't find the character '\'. Instead it will look for the character '\' which follows it. To search for a '\' we would use:

```
/\\/
```

## Searching for text

The sequence:

```
/string/
```

by itself, searches for a line containing 'string' and prints it out on the terminal. For example:

```
/He/
He jested, quaffed and swore;
```

Note that the current line after a search is set to the last line found, which in this instance is also the first occurrence of a line containing the specified string. Searches 'wrap around' the ends of a file, so that if there is only one such line to be found, and the current line when you give the search command is already greater than the line number you are seeking, it will be found. This is a convenient convention; on the other hand, if you are looking for the first occurrence of a string in the file, rather than the next occurrence, you have to return to the start of the file before beginning the search.

We can combine the /..../ construction with the  s  command to search for a line containing a string and then change another string in the same line: e.g.

```
/drunken/s/private/colonel/p
A drunken colonel of the Buffs
```

Since the current line is now line 3, if we want to find the first instance of the string 'He', we must return to line 1, by typing:

```
1
Last night, among his fellow roughs,
```

We can now search for the first occurrence of 'He';

```
/He/
He jested, quaffed and swore;
```

Repeated searches for a string can be carried out by omitting the string from subsequent /..../ commands:

```
/He/
He jested, quaffed and swore;
//
He stands in Elgin's place:
//
He yet can call his own
//
He only knows that not through him
```

## Global search

If you want to find every occurence of a string it can be done by putting a 'global' argument, 'g' at the beginning of the command:

```
g/He/p
He jested, quaffed and swore;
He stands in Elgin's place:
He yet can call his own.
He only knows that not through him
```

The 'g' flag has a different significance within a line from its meaning between lines. For example, if you want to alter all the occurrences of a string in a line, you should use 'g' after the search command; otherwise only the first occurrence will be amended: e.g.

```
1
Last night, among his fellow roughs,
s/a/b/gp
Lbst night, bmong his fellow roughs,
```

This has altered both 'a' characters in the line; while the following command:

```
s/b/a/p
Last night, bmong his fellow roughs,
```

has only corrected the first one. It requires another command:

```
s/b/a/p
Last night, among his fellow roughs,
```

to restore the whole line. If the 'g' is omitted, then the effect of a search and substitute command across a range of line numbers is simply to alter the first occurrence of the string in each line where it is found:

```
1,2s/a/b/p
1,2p
Lbst night, among his fellow roughs,
He jested, qubffed and swore;
```

A second command would alter the next occurring instances of the string:

```
1,2s/a/b/p
Lbst night, bmong his fellow roughs,
He jested, qubffed bnd swore;
```

while a single command using the 'g' flag will restore both lines:

```
1,2s/b/a/g
1,2p
```
Last night, among his fellow roughs,
He jested, quaffed and swore;


## Matching characters

The editor provides a number of characters with special meanings in search and replace commands. The character '.' in the context of a search command means any character will be matched to the '.' character if it used in a search string. For example, to look for the string 'a' followed by any character followed by 'd', we give the command:

```
/a.d/
```
He stands in Elgin's place:

Repeated use of this search command will produce all the other instances of the sequence:

```
//
```
Bewildered and alone,
```
//
```
Shall England come to shame.
```
//
```
He jested, quaffed and swore;
```
//
```
He stands in Elgin's place:

Note the wrap-around effect, brought about by the finishing point of the previous command. Since '.' means 'any character', it can be used to mean 'the first character in a line'. In the following command:

```
1
```
Last night, among his fellow roughs,
```
s/./P/p
```
Past night, among his fellow roughs,

we search for any character and substitute a 'P' for it. This works because the first character of the line was, coincidentally, the character which we wanted to amend.


### Finding the first character of a line

If we want to find the first character in a line irrespective of context within the line we should use the special character '^'. The following puts a parenthesis at the start of the line:

104

```
s/^/(/p
```
(Past night, among his fellow roughs,


## Finding the last character in a line

Conversely, the symbol for 'last character in the line' is '$'. To insert a right parenthesis at the end of the line we would use:

```
s/$/)/p
```
(Past night, among his fellow roughs,)


## Special characters in search and replace

To handle a specific character which has a special meaning attached to it you would, of course, use the '\' before it. This has the effect of depriving it of any special meaning it may otherwise have had. Thus, for instance, to change the commas to periods in the line we would say:

```
s/,/\./g
```
(Past night. among his fellow roughs.)


## Forcing a match

An alternative use for the characters '^' and '$' is to use them as part of a string to be matched. When used in this way they will force a match at the start or end of a line. For example:

```
/^A/p
```
A drunken colonel of the Buffs

finds the next line which begins with the character 'A' (as distinct from the next line containing an 'A').

The next special character of interest is '★' which means 'as many of the preceding characters as possible'. It can be used, for example, to remove a number of repeated characters from a line. The command

```
s/ *//
```

would remove as many successive spaces as it found from the current line. If used in conjunction with the '.' character in a search, we can specify the whole of a line, since '.' means 'any character'. Thus the command:

```
s/.*/New line/p
New line
```

replaces the whole of the current line with a new one. This type of command will nearly always succeed in altering a line, since '*' means zero or more occurrences of the preceding character, the expression /?*/ will always produce a match, whatever the value of '?'. The deletion of characters can be stopped by terminating the search string with a particular, expected, character. For example, to edit the current line to remove all but the last character we can use:

```
s/.*n//p
e
```

## Matching strings

The character '&' can be used in a replace string to mean 'the string which was matched by the search string'. For example:

```
2
He jested, quaffed and swore;
s/He/& often/p
He often jested, quaffed and swore;
```

The '&' can save typing in a long search string again, e.g.

```
u
1,$s/He often jested, quaffed and swore/& and then he
spat upon the floor/p
He often jested, quaffed and swore and then he spat
upon the floor;
```

## Character sets

A set of characters to be searched for can be specified by including them between square brackets '[' and ']'. Let us return to line 1 and try this out:

```
1
Last night, among his fellow roughs,
```

If we give the command:

```
s/[atih,]/x/p
Lxst night, among his fellow roughs,
```

then the first character of the set 'atih' is changed to an 'x'. If now we
give the global command:

```
s//x/gp
Lxsx nxgxxx xmong xxs fellow rougxsx
```

then all the characters in the previously specified set have an 'x'
substituted for them. It is possible to use the characters '[' and ']' in the
set of characters between brackets, thus:

```
s/x/[/gp
L[s[ n[g[[[ [mong [[s fellow roug[s[
s/[[]/y/gp
Lysy nygyyy ymong yys fellow rougysy
s/y/]/gp
L]s] n]g]]] ]mong ]]s fellow roug]s]
s/[]]/z/gp
Lzsz nzgzzz zmong zzs fellow rougzsz
```

The only restriction on the use of the brackets in searches is that if
you are looking for a right bracket, ']', it must be the first character in
the class between brackets. The left bracket '[' is not special in any way
and can be used freely. (When you think about the way the command
has to be implemented, the reasons behind this become clear.)

## Character ranges

As well as searching for specific characters it is possible to search for a
range of characters using the square bracket construction. In the
following example, the characters in lower case between 'a' and 'z'
inclusive are searched for and changed to the character '2':

```
s/[a-z]/2/gp
L222 222222 22222 222 222222 2222222
```

## Excluding a range

You can exclude a range of characters as well as including them. This
is done by putting a ' ^ ' character before the range of characters to be
excluded from the search, e.g.

```
s/[^A-Z]/3/gp
L333333333333333333333333333333333
```

Once again, the special case where you want to exclude the

character '^' from a search is catered for. The '^' character has no special meaning except at the start of a string. In the following:

```
s/L/^/p
^333333333333333333333333333333333333
/[^^]/p
He jested, quaffed and swore;
```

the first line found is one not starting with a '^'.

## 6.2  The Screen Editor

The screen editor in most frequent use is called *vi* which means visual interactive editor.

*vi* is not a particularly versatile example of its kind. In most popular screen oriented text handling programs, specially designated function keys carry out the editing commands. This means that the alphanumeric keyboard can be used for the usual purpose of text input.

Because UNIX has to be standardised across so many terminal types *vi* uses ordinary keys for unusual purposes, i.e. giving commands to the editor. This is a solution which is neither popular with the user who is seeking a versatile screen editor, nor with the programmer, who will continue to use *ed*. However a brief account of the ways of *vi* will be given here for those who may wish to use it.

### Terminal Type

In order to use the screen editor the system must first know what kind of terminal it is dealing with. If it does not know this already you should tell it by giving the shell command:

```
$ TERM=<terminal type> export TERM
```

### Invoking *vi*

*vi* is invoked by the command:

```
$ vi <filename>
```

### Screen display

If the filename given is that of a new file this command will produce a display like this on the terminal:

108

```
~
~
~
~
~
~
~
~
~
~
.
.
.
.
"filename"[new file]
```

If the filename is of an existing file, then the first few lines of the file will be displayed on the screen. Editing of the file may now be carried out.

## Quitting

To leave the screen editor type

    `:q`

(you will notice that commands preceded by ':' appear on the bottom line of the display.)

If you have not written the contents of the file out the editor will warn you of the fact. To leave *vi* regardless of the status of the file, type

    `:q!`

and this will force the quit.

## Commands

The commands used by *vi* are fundamentally the same in operation as those of *ed*. However the way in which they are given is different, usually involving the use of control characters or the ':' (colon) character. The effects of the commands can be seen on the terminal screen as they are performed.

## Inserting text

To insert text the command

i

is given. Text, including return characters, can now be freely typed in and will appear on the screen.

When you want to terminate the input you type an escape character.

If text is to be appended to existing text rather than inserted before it, the command

a

should be used. The distinction should already be familiar from the use of *ed*. The material is placed before the cursor when inserting, after the cursor when appending.

## Cursor positioning

To view parts of the file, the cursor position can be moved back and forward, up and down. For this purpose the control characters are used. (Pressing the control key together with another key is represented here by ˆ ).

ˆF

moves the display forward through the file by a full screen height. Moving back a full screen is done by means of

ˆB

To move half a screen forward use

ˆD

and to move half a screen back use

ˆU

(These can be remembered by the initial letters of 'back', 'forward', 'up' and 'down'.)

The cursor can be moved about on the screen by means of the following commands:

### Major moves

Moving to 'Home', i.e. the first line of the screen:

ˆH

Moving to the last line of the screen can be done by

**^L**

Moving to the middle of the screen is

**^M**

*Little moves*

| | |
|---|---|
| **<space>** or **l** | moves one place to the right |
| **<backspace>** or **h** | moves one place to the left |
| **k** | move up one place |
| **j** | move down one place |
| **$** | moves at the end of the line |
| **+** | moves to the start of the next line |
| **-** | moves to the start of the previous line. |
| **w** | moves forward to the beginning of the next word |
| **b** | moves back to the start of the previous word |
| **e** | moves forward to the end of the current word |

## Deleting and changing text

To delete the character before the cursor, you simply do

**x**

If you want to delete several characters you type the number n before the command:

**nx**

Deleting a word is carried out by means of

**dw**

This removes the current word, i.e. the one which the cursor is located in or after.

The whole of the current line is deleted by the command

**dd**

and the remainder of a line in front of the cursor can be deleted by

**d**

Replacing a character is carried out by means of the command

`r<c>`

where c is the character to be substituted for the one the cursor is at.
The current word is changed by means of the command

`cw`

followed by an escape character.
To change the rest of the line, use

`c`

The input sequence is again terminated by an escape character.
A way of moving text from one place to another is provided by the *yank* command.

`y`

This yanks (copies) the current line into a buffer, from which it can be copied to a new cursor position by means of the

`P`

or *pull* command.

It is obviously desirable to be able to deal in variable units of text size, and these can be specified by means of what are called 'objects'.

An example of an object is a character, a word or a line. Most commands we have looked at contain an object either implicitly (they work on a character) or explcitly (e.g. delete the current word).

It is possible to specify the object to be used in any command according to the following set of conventions:

| | |
|---|---|
| c | the current character |
| w | the current word |
| ( | the start of the current sentence |
| ) | the end of the current sentence |
| { | the start of the current paragraph |
| } | the end of the current paragraph |

## Searching

If you need to find a piece of text you can use the search facility. As in the *ed* the sequence to be found is placed between slash characters /.../ so that the command

`/oqwrx/`

will locate the cursor at the start of the string. Again, as in *ed* the sequence ?...? searches backwards instead of forwards for the string between the queries.

## 6.3  Text Formatting

A very useful feature of the UNIX system is the ability to produce documents formatted in a particular way. This can save a lot of effort in the attempt to produce readable documentation, taking care of such things as justification of text (aligning it with the borders), spacing it, providing indents and headings and so on.

There are a number of formatting tools available within UNIX. These cover a variety of needs, including simple text formatting capabilities and extending to the typesetting of mathematical formulae and utilities for driving a phototypesetter.

## Roff

We will start with the simplest of them, called *roff*. *roff* formats text by means of embedded control lines which specify what formatting operation is to be carried out. These control lines consist of requests for particular operations followed by parameters specifying the quantities involved. For example, the line:

```
.bl 6
```

consists of a request for blank lines to be inserted into the text, followed by the number of lines to be spaced. This request would be placed between two chunks of text which were to be separated by space, the whole text looking like this:

```
[text]
.bl 6
[more text]
```

Each request thus has a line to itself, beginning with a period character, '.'. In this tutorial the examples will all be indented, because this text is itself being prepared in a version of *roff*, and the indent prevents the example control lines from affecting the text, but in actual use the period would be the first character in the line.

## Page format

The first thing to do when preparing text for formatting is to input the control lines necessary for the overall control of the page format. The request:

.bp

begins a new page on the printing device. If we give a number of pages, e.g.

.bp <n>

we can skip several pages. The default value of 'n' is 1, however, so that '.bp' gives us a new page.

## *Page Length*

It is now a good idea to set the page length and line length if these are different from the default values. The request:

```
.pl 50
.ll 45
```

will set the page length to 50 lines and the line length to 45 characters respectively. If we do nothing at this stage we will get the default values of 66 lines of 65 characters. These values are good for many printers, but it is as well to know your own output device and its characteristics thoroughly before attempting to format text for it. Terminals are another device which must be suited by the formatting process, even if they are only used to check the output before committing yourself to paper. Discover the number of characters which will fit on the screen in one line and keep your lines within this limit.

## Document headings

You will now want to have some kind of heading for your document. Suppose we are going to write a text about macro processor commands in UNIX. We could give the document the following header request:

.he??? MACRO PROCESSORS IN UNIX

## An example of *roff*

In order to illustrate some of the requests we have been discussing,

here is a document in two forms. The document represents a testi-
monial for a student applying for employment. First, the *roff* input,
containing the embedded control lines needed to produce the final
version, and second the formatted version as output from *roff*.

```
·$ ed ref
ref?
a
.bp 1
.ro
.pl 30
.ll 60
.in 30
.na
School of Colateral Studies
University of Barchester,
Little Glebe Lane,
HOLLERTON.
HB2 7UP.
18.07.82
.bl 2
.in 0
.ce 2
To Whom It May Concern
.bl 3
Hannah Chasuble Hardcastle
.bl 2
.ad
.hy 1
ti5
Miss Hardcastle has been known to me for
the last three years as a student on the
B.Sc. Associated Studies degree
which we teach.
My contact with her was limited for the
first year to tutorial advice,
as I do not myself teach in that year.
In the second and third years I taught
her in three courses: Perception of Cultural Change,
Computer Methods in Social Science and
Sword-Swallowing, which was her Option subject.
2
She is a well, mannered girl,
liked by the majority of her fellows and by
many of the staff.
I have always found her completely honest.
.
w
q
·???
$ roff ref
```

```
School of Colateral Studies
University of Barchester,
Little Glebe Lane,
HOLLERTON.
HB2 7UP.
18.07.82
```

To Whom It May Concern

Hannah Chasuble Hardcastle

Miss Hardcastle has been known to me for the last three years as a student on the B.Sc. Associated Studies degree which we teach. My contact with her was limited for the first year to tutorial advice, as I do not myself teach in that year. In the second and third years I taught her in three courses: Perception of Cultural Change, Computer Methods in Social Science and Sword-Swallowing, which was her Option subject.

She is a well, mannered girl, liked by the majority of her fellows and by many of the staff. I have always found her completely honest.

## troff and nroff

Two more versions of *roff, troff* and *nroff*, also handle formatting for output. The *nroff/troff* command has the form:

```
$ { nroff } [options] [files]
$ { troff }
```

The options for both commands include page numbering, selective printing of certain page numbers only, handling read insertions and prepending a macro file. The *nroff* and *troff* commands have certain options which they share and certain options which are peculiar to each.

The *nroff* command has the options of specifying the output terminal name and using the tab stops on the terminal. The *troff* command options allow the user to direct output to the terminal (standard output), to print using a single point-size for speed of output, reporting on the status of the typesetter and waiting until it is ready.

The options for the *nroff* and *troff* commands must be specified separately, not together as is allowed in most commands, e.g.

```
$ nroff -T37 -o2,4,6,8
```

## 6.4   File Processing Commands

We have already seen in Chapter 2 some of the simpler commands for handling files. There are a number of more sophisticated tools for this purpose which we will turn to now.

## Regular expressions

The following commands all have in common the fact that they operate on something called 'regular expressions'. This they share with the *ed* command. The concept of a regular expression will therefore first be explained.

A regular expression is a way of defining a string, or strings, of characters. This is done by writing a regular expression which matches the desired string(s).

## Syntax rules

The syntax of regular expressions is rigorous, and in cases of doubt reference should be made to the formal definition given in the UNIX Programmer's Manual. The following however are some of the main rules:

1   A string of characters will match exactly that string,
    e.g.    tram   will match  'tram'
2   A '\' character followed by a character will match that character,
    e.g.    \&   will match  '&'
This is useful when dealing with characters which have special functions, but which you want to treat literally on a particular occasion.
3   A '.' will match any character,
    e.g.    .ram   matches   'cram', 'dram', 'gram', etc.
4   A character string preceded by '^' matches a string starting at the beginning of a line. A string ending in '$' matches one ending at the end of a line.
5   Character strings in square brackets '[ ]' match a range of characters.
    e.g.    [A-Z]   matches anything in the range A to Z.
In general, regular expressions are sensitive to case. Ranges are worked out in ASCII sequence. Abbreviations like [a–z 0–9] can be used.

**6**  A string followed by '+' matches one or more such successive strings,

e.g.     tom+   matches   'tom' or 'tomtom'

A string followed by '★' matches 0 or more such expressions in succession.

e.g.     tom★   matches   '  ', 'tom' or 'tomtom'


## 6.5   Pattern Recognition and Processing – *awk*

The command *awk* provides the facilities of a pattern recognition and processing language. It is invoked by:

```
$ awk <program> <file>
```

What *awk*  does is to take the lines of an input file and process them according to the program.

The input file is treated as a series of lines divided into fields. The lines are normally separated by newline characters, and the fields by spaces. The fields are known by the names of the parameters $1, $2,... $0.

The program is like a C program in format (see Chapter 5). It can either be given explicitly or else it can be taken from a file. It consists of a series of statements, and each statement specifies a pattern and an action to be taken when the pattern is recognised.


### Relational expressions

The patterns are combinations of regular expressions and relational expressions. Regular expressions are the same as those used by *ed*, and are a convenient way of specifying character patterns. Relational expressions are conditions involving the use of such relations as '>', '<=', etc. as in the C programming language.

For example, we might write:

```
$ awk if $1>$2 print $2 afile
```

This would take the lines of 'file', look at the first and second fields of each one, compare them and print the second field if the first was greater than the second. The comparison is done lexicographically, i.e. in ASCII sequence by default, though other lexicographic sequences can be defined.

## Program files

A program file can offer great flexibility about actions. The general form of a program is:

```
BEGIN { initial statements
}
selector   { action }
...
END     { final statements
}
```

Programs can use the following features of C: assignment statements, *if, while, for, break, continue, print, printf, next* and *exit*. Statements can be ordered in the same way as in C using newlines and braces as separators.

Functions available are *sqrt, log, exp, int, length*(s) (giving the length of its argument), *substr* (s,m,n) (returning the string n characters long starting at the mth character), and *index*(s,t) (giving the position of the first occurrence of t in s).

The field and line separators of the input can be altered from the default values if required by altering the values of the shell variables FS and RS respectively. There are other shell variables which can be accessed also, for example NF which gives the number of fields in the current record, and NR which gives the number of records in a file.

All in all, *awk* is a very useful command, especially to the systems programmer.

## 6.6   The Stream Editor – *sed*

Another facility for file processing, which is in some ways similar to *awk*, is *sed*, the stream editor. It is invoked by:

```
$ sed -e <script>
```

or by:

```
$ sed -f <scriptfile>
```

The first form of the command takes requests from 'script' and processes them against the input. The second form takes the requests from a script file.

*sed* processes the standard input against a series of requests specified in 'script'. It can also of course be redirected to carry out automatic editing of a file.

## Requests in *Sed*

Requests are like the comamnds given in *ed* and are of the form

```
address1, address2 request arguments
```

The addresses are interpreted to give a range of line values, as they are by the editor. If they are omitted then the request is applied to every line of the file.

The requests are again like those of the *ed* command. They include *a* (append), *b* (branch to a label), *c* (change), *d* (delete), *i* (insert), *l* (list), *p* (print), *q* (quit), *r* (read), *w* (write) and the *s* (substitute) request based on regular expressions. Labelling is done by prepending ':label' to a line.

There are also requests to enable editing to proceed without intervention by giving explicit requests. Some of these are requests for input and output such as *n* (copy input to output), *P* (copy input to output up to the next newline) and *N* (append the next line of input with an embedded newline).

There is also a *t* (test) request which branches to a label in the event of a substitution having been made. This gives the programmer more flexibility about actions. There is also a hold space which can be used for moving chunks of text around.

## 6.7   Lexical Analysis Program Generator – *lex*

The aim of *lex* is to enable a filter program to be written, i.e. one operating on the input. The nature of filters was discussed in Chapter 4. A filter is a program operating on an input stream and transforming it in some way before output. An example of a filter is the *tr* command which translates specified character sets in the input into others in the output stream.

## Program specification

A *lex* program specification is written by giving rules for what is to be done in the event of certain strings being encountered in the input.

The general form of a *lex* program is:

```
definitions
%%
rules
%%
user subroutines
```

There are often no definitions and subroutines. The bulk of the program is therefore made up of the rules, which are of the form:

```
<expression>    <action>
```

where the expression is a regular expression, i.e. an input pattern requiring recognition, and the action is a statement in the C programming language (although other programming langauges could be specified).

For example, the *lex* program script:

```
%%
spell printf("Name starts\n");
unspell printf("Name ends\n");
```

will look for the strings 'spell' and 'unspell' in the input and print messages when it finds them. All other input will be copied to the output unaltered.

## Definitions

The first section, definitions, can be used for setting up actions which are to be used in the main body of the rules section, and associating names with them. These actions can then be referred to by name later.

For example, the definition:

```
D  [0-9]
```

would associate the name 'D' with the digits in the range 0 to 9. This name could then be used in the program section

```
D  [0-9]
.
.
%%
{D}+  printf("Integer\n");
.
.
```

## Subroutines

The subroutines section is for any additional routines which the user may need to call.

## Invoking and compiling *lex*

When the command:

```
$ lex <file>
```

is given, a program is generated from the file and is put into *lex.yy.c*.

## Compilation

This program can then be compiled by giving the command:

```
$ cc lex.yy.c
```

The executable program will then be put into *a.out* in the usual way. *lex* can be used in conjunction with the input language analyser, *yacc* (see next section).

## 6.8 Input Structuring Program – *yacc*

The name *yacc* is an acronym for 'Yet Another Compiler-Compiler', but this does not fully explain its function. *yacc* is a tool for specifying rules which will analyse and check input data. In order to do this, *yacc* produces a parser which scans the input, and it is this 'compiler-compiling' nature of the utility which gives it its name.

To understand the function of *yacc*, suppose that data fields in the input to a program are supposed to have a given format. It is obviously desirable that the data be checked through the program before being operated on, to make sure that they are in this correct format. If they are not, the data can then be either re-input or skipped.

Such an application would be suitable for *yacc*. Other applications might be the analysis of mathematical formulae for typesetting or checking programs for errors of syntax. What all such applications have in common is that, in each of them, the input has a certain grammatical structure and this grammar must be in some way determined or checked in order to decide what to do.

### Operation of *yacc*

*Yacc* works by creating a parser, which knows the rules for the input grammar and applies them. In order to do this it must also know what symbols to look for in the input stream. These can be defined by means of a lexical analyser, which is used in conjunction with the parser. Such a lexical analyser may be written as part of the *yacc* specification. Alternatively it may be written using *lex*, which we have already discussed.

The lexical analyser divides the input stream up into *tokens*. These are symbols or strings of symbols having a specific meaning to the program, such as digits, letters, brackets, etc. The parser operates on these using the rules laid down.

## Format of a *yacc* specification file

A *yacc* specification file has the following format:

```
declarations
%%
grammar rules
%%
programs
```

## Declarations

The declarations section is for a varety of purposes. In the first place it is used for introducing C routines which may need to be included, such as *stdio.h*. Again, it is used for declarations of the usual C variety (declarations of the type of variables, structures etc.)

Additionally, the declarations section is where the user defines token names, which are to be used by the later sections.

## Grammar rules

The rules section lays down the grammar rules which will be built into the parser. Rules are strings of letters and non-initial numbers, separated by spaces and punctuation marks, e.g.

```
A  :   B C ;
```

This means, roughly speaking, that an 'A' is defined as a 'B' followed by a 'C'. A concrete example might be:

```
number   :   number digit ;
```

which says that a number is a number followed by a number or a digit (note the element of recursion in this definition.)

## Actions

The grammar rules can have actions associated with them. The actions are written in a subset of C, and are specified by following the grammar rule by the action, e.g.

```
A   :     B C ;
          { printf("Message\n"); }
```

which will print 'Message' when an 'A' occurs.

Grammar rules can be written successively like this:

```
number   :      digit
                number  digit
         ;
```

## Program section

The program section is for the program which defines the lexical analyser. The lexical analyser is necessary to define to *yacc* what the 'tokens' are on which its grammar rules are based. The program will look at the input stream and identify symbols in it and these will be used as the atoms out of which the syntactical structure is built.

## Implementation of *yacc*

The *yacc* specification is turned into a C program which parses the input according to the rules given. This process is done by the parser working as a finite state machine with a stack. The current state is on top of the stack and the parser can read the next token ahead. Based on this knowledge the parser takes one of four actions at each stage: it can shift (substitute a new current state by pushing down the stack), reduce (when the right hand side of a grammar rule is reached the rule is complete and the stack is popped an appropriate number of times), accept (end of input) or give an error.

## Invoking *yacc*

The command

```
$ yacc
```

produces a file called *y.tab.c* which can be compiled by the C compiler to produce a program *yyparse*. This must be loaded with other routines, including error routines, to give the executable *yacc* program.

# 7 Use and Superuse

So far we have been looking at commands which may be given and carried out by any user on a UNIX system. Powerful as these commands are, there are some others which are not accessible to the ordinary user – mainly those connected with maintenance of the system itself. These commands can be carried out only at the request of a special user, called the superuser, who is in effect the system manager. This chapter will be concerned with superusers and the commands available to them.

## 7.1 The Need for a Superuser

In any multi-user system, something like a superuser must exist, even though they may not be called by that name. It is fairly clear why this must be so: someone must be capable of maintaining and altering the system, if only in order to put things right when they go wrong. It is also clear that in a system of any size not every user can be permitted such facilities. Not all users are equally competent, or equally scrupulous, and deliberate or inadvertant interference with the system will sooner or later result in innocent users getting 'bombed'.

There is in fact usually more than one person who is able to tamper with the system, though in UNIX there is only one superuser identity as far as the system checks are concerned. In practice more than one person is likely to know the superuser password and be able to sign on as the superuser. A sensible number of people who may become the superuser is perhaps two – the nominal system manager and a deputy. To extend the facility of superuse beyond this weakens the concept of a superuser class.

On occasions it may be possible for ordinary users to be given superuser facilities; these can be given on a temporary basis only by manipulating the password.

There are two main types of activity which the superuser may be required to carry out; maintaining the system and its files, and coordinating use of the system among the individuals allowed to sign on. There are thus two main classes of commands associated with the superuser: those concerned with the system, particularly the file system, and those concerned with other users and their needs. We shall look at these in turn.

## 7.2 Signing on as Superuser

To sign on as the superuser you must first know the superuser password. You then follow one of two methods. If you are logging in to the system, you respond to the request to login in the usual way, using the identifier 'root' and the superuser password:

```
login:  root
password:  [superuser password]
£
```

The password is not echoed by the system for security reasons.

### The *su* command

If you are already signed on, you can become the superuser by means of the command  *su*. The dialogue would look like this:

```
$  su
password:  [superuser password]
£
```

### Superuser prompt symbol

In both cases the system prompts the superuser with a different prompt symbol (commonly '£') to indicate their superuser status.

In fact the superuser needs reminding of his powers as much as possible, since they are all but unlimited. Once you are the superuser you can create and destroy file systems, admit new users and remove existing ones from the system, remove files and directories regardless of permission, etc. It is clearly in everyone's interests that such powers are used with due caution.

## 7.3 Adding New Users

One of the primary tasks which the superuser will have to carry out is adding new users to the system. The first user he adds is probably himself under his own identifier. How is this done?

## Adding a user to /etc/passwd

Let's suppose that we are faced with a new file system with no users (except *root*) and we want to add a user called *dick*. In order to do this we have to do two things. Firstly, we have to edit the file which contains user passwords, adding Dick's password, so that the system will recognise him when he signs on. This is done as follows:

```
£ ed /etc/passwd
208
```

If we list the file /etc/passwd we will see some strange looking entries:

```
1,$p
root::0:1::/:
daemon:x:1:1::/:
cron:x:1:1::/:
sys::2:2::/sys:
bin::3:3::/bin:
uucp::4:4::/usr/lib/uucp:uucico
dmr::7:3::/usr/dmr:
who::8:8::/bin:sync
unix::10:10::/:
```

Within each entry there are a number of fields, each field containing a certain piece of information. Fields are separated by a colon ':'. A null entry is denoted by two colons in succession '::'.

The first entry is the identifier of the user. The second entry is his password, which appears in encrypted form only, and hence cannot be read by anyone in its original (and only usable) form.

When adding a new user to the system it is usual to set his password field to null and let him assign a password when he first signs on. (Alternatively you can give him a password known to only the super-user and the new user, since a null field means that anyone can sign on with the identifier alone.)

The third and fourth entries are the user id and the group id, which are assigned by the system manager. The final entry is the working directory, which is normally /usr/login name.

When the system is fresh, the only users are certain 'daemons', which are processes running to keep the system active and useful, such as *root* and *cron*. To add *dick* to the system we would do the following operations:

127

```
.1
unix::10:10::/:
a
dick::20:20::/usr/dick:
w
209
q
£
```

## Adding the new user's directory

You must now do another thing – make a directory called */usr/dick*.

```
£ mkdir /usr/dick
£
```

This directory is Dick's login directory, and can be seen if we list the contents of **/usr** :

```
£ ls -l /usr
total 21
drwxrwxrwx 2 bin         80 Jul 13 01:00 adm
drwxrwxrwx 2 bin       1712 Jul 13 01:10 bin
drwxr-xr-x 2 root        32 Sep 22 21:50 dick
.
.
.
```

The new user is now added to the system. You can test this by logging in under the new user id:

```
login: dick
$
```

## Setting up for a new user

At this stage some of the shell parameters should be set by means of the *set* command. If we do a *set* without argument we can see what values these are currently set to.

```
$ set
HOME=/
IFS=

PATH=:/bin:/usr/bin
PS1=$
PS2=>
$
```

These parameters are used by the shell when interpreting commands. The first parameter, HOME, gives the user's home or login directory. This should normally be */usr/[identifier]*.

The parameter IFS specifies the characters which are to be treated by the shell as internal field separators. Usually these are the characters blank, tab and newline. Since these are non-printing, except for the newline, all that appears on the screen is a blank line.

The parameter PATH gives the sequence of directories which are to be searched for the names of commands (i.e. programs). The directories specified are separated by the character ':', and the name of the first directory is preceded by ':'.

In the above case the shell will first look in */bin* for the command name, and then it will look in */usr/bin*. It is quite easy to specify directories to be included in the search. For example, if you want to use a command which is held in */etc* then this can be done by specifying:

```
$ PATH=:/bin:/usr/bin:/etc
```

## Exporting shell parameters

The parameter must also be exported to the shell so that it knows about it, by:

```
$ export PATH
```

It is now possible to give more directly the command:

```
$ [command]
```

rather than

```
$ /etc/[command]
```

## Home directory in search path

Again, it is sensible to include the user's home directory in the path to be searched, since you will want some of your own program names to be interpreted as commands by the shell when you are logged in. This could be done for *dick* by:

```
$ PATH=:/bin:/usr/bin:/etc:/usr/dick
```

129

## Prompt characters

The remaining parameters, PS1 and PS2, give the string prompt characters, that is, the characters which will be printed to prompt the user for input. Where only one string is expected, as in most commands, this character is the value of PS1, initially set to '$'. If any further input is required, subsequent lines will be prompted by the PS2 character '>'.

These prompt characters can be set to any required values, including string values, so that users can remind themselves of who they are by altering their primary string prompt, say to:

```
$ PS1=dick$
```

they will then be reasonably sure that when they see the prompt:

```
dick$
```

that they are signed in at that terminal. (It can sometimes be confusing, if a number of terminals and identities are in use, just who is signed on where. You can always find out by giving the command:

```
$ who am I
dick tty01Nov 6 11:40
```

which will tell you.)


## MAIL parameter

There are a number of other parameters which can be set by the system manager or by the user. One very useful one is MAIL, which specifies the file in which mail will be put for the user. If this parameter is set then the shell will tell the user each time he signs on that there is mail for him:

```
you have mail
```

The mail file is usually */usr/mail/[identifier]*. The parameter MAIL should thus be set:

```
$ MAIL=/usr/mail/dick; export MAIL
```

If we list */usr* we will now find an entry something like this:

```
drwxr-xr-x 2 root          32 Sep 22 21:22 dick
```

This entry indicates that there is a user whose identifier is *dick* and it also shows that the owner of this directory is *root* (since root created it). Since *root* owns */usr/dick*, Dick will find that he has not got full control over 'his' files.

## Changing ownership of home directory

Dick will find that there are many things he cannot do with his own home directory, because currently he doesn't have write permission for it. One of the things which the superuser ought to do for Dick is to give him ownership of his home directory. This is done by means of the *chown* command.

    *chown* changes the ownership of files so that they partake of the permissions open to their new owner (and their group) rather than their old one. The superuser may thus do:

```
£ chown dick /usr/dick
```

which effectively does the required job. (The command *chgrp* can be used to change the group ownership of the specified file. This is sometimes of value for files used by a particular set of users.)

## 7.4 Removing Users

Removing users from the system (for whatever reason!) is the inverse of the above process. Deleting the user's password from the file */etc/passwd* will effectively prevent signing on, though in other ways (e.g. for accounting daemons) the user will continue to exist. To make a user into an unperson his home directory must be removed by means of the command:

```
£ rm -r /usr/dick
```

## Recursive emptying

The option '-r' means that files are recursively emptied and removed, starting with the directory */usr/dick*. Thus, if there are any directories within */usr/dick* these will be emptied first, and so on. Other odds and ends may also need to be tidied up, such as links to other files, but this process should be automatic provided none of Dick's files are required but have no links formed to them. Only when the link count at the i-node of a file reduces to zero does that file cease to exist in the file system.

## 7.5 System Startup

The superuser has certain responsibilities to the system when starting it up for the first time, or when restarting it after a shutdown has occurred. Let us look now at the sequence of events from the time of switch-on to getting a UNIX system up and running in multi-user mode.

Having switched on the computer, the first thing to do is to load the UNIX resident from whatever medium it is held on. Let us assume for the sake of example that the machine is a PDP-II/34 and that the UNIX resident is held on RL02 disk. The procedure is to boot the II/34, by pressing CNTRL/HLT and CNTRL/BOOT, producing some such print out as this:

```
111266 000200 077160 002770
@
```

This is the usual print out of registers given by an II/34 after booting. It is now waiting for a two letter media code followed by the name of the UNIX resident program. We will assume the following:

```
@DYunix
mem = 180928
£
```

The line beginning 'mem =' tells the operator how much memory is available for user programs. You have now started UNIX in single user mode and some checks are ready to be done.

The above is only an example of how to bring up a UNIX system, and the details will vary depending on the hardware used. In general, the procedure to follow is to boot the computer and then boot the UNIX resident from its hardware (usually disk or tape). In practice, naturally, this can be more or less complicated depending on the arrangements made for the installation in question. Reference to the manufacturer's information will be essential in all cases.

## 7.6 System Checks

After start up the system is initially running in single-user mode. Checks of the file system and of the devices attached to it should now be carried out before the system is allowed to go into multi-user mode.

## Checking integrity of file system

The first and most important check is of the integrity of the file system, and this is carried out by the *icheck* command as follows:

```
£ icheck /dev/root
/dev/root:
files    1718  (r=1600,d=99,b=7,c=12)
used    16358  (i=333,ii=15,iii=0,d=15895)
free     1396
missing     0
£
```

This printout will now be explained. The file system is addressed as */dev/root*. The first line of the printout tells you the total number of files and the number of regular, directory, block special and character special files.

The second line gives the total number of blocks in use and the number of single, double and triple indirectly addressed blocks, and the number of directly addressed blocks. The next lines give the number of free blocks and the number of blocks missing, that is, the number of blocks not appearing to be either in a file or on the free list, which is a list of available blocks kept in the super-block of the file system.

### Bad blocks

Bad blocks will be picked up by the *icheck* command and the i-node number and the type of fault will be given.

The *icheck* command can be used with the option '-s', which will cause the system to ignore the super-block information about the number of free blocks and rewrite the super-block. After this operation the file system should be rebooted.

### Locating blocks

The option '–b' followed by block numbers can be used to get a listing of where particular blocks are.

## Directory consistency check

Another important system check is the *dcheck* or directory consistency check. The *dcheck* command reads the directories in the file system and compares the link-count at the i-node of each file with the number of times that the file appears in directories. These two quantities should be equal. If no discrepancy arises then the command prints out the file system directory name and terminates:

```
£ dcheck /dev/root
/dev/root:
```

If there is a discrepancy then details of the i-node link count and number of entries in directories is printed for each case in i-number order:

```
£ dcheck /dev/root
/dev/root:
        entries   link cnt
99         16        17
281         0         0
```

## Clearing i-nodes

If an error does occur then it may be possible to put it right without tampering with i-nodes. However the i-nodes may need to be cleared in some circumstances.

Suppose for example that a directory has been accidentally lost, and that the file had no other directory entries. The number of entries for a file in that directory will be reduced to zero as far as the *dcheck* is concerned, but will remain the same in the file's i-node. It may then be necessary to reallocate the i-node, and the only way of doing this is to remove the old i-node, because the file itself has now disappeared. If the discrepancy has come about through corruption of the i-node itself, then again it may have to be removed.

For these reasons the superuser is given the power to remove i-nodes by means of the *clri* command:

```
£ clri 1676
```

Although it can be seen that this is a necessary power of the superuser, it will be readily appreciated that it is not one to be abused.

The circumstances under which i-nodes should be cleared are not always easy to define. In general however the rule is if an i-node refers to a file which no longer exists then it may be safely cleared. If however there is no i-node for a file then preferably the file itself should be got rid of.

## Finding i-numbers for files

It is of course necessary when dealing with the i-nodes to know the i-number corresponding to filenames, and vice versa.

We can find out the i-node of a file from the listing of the directory containing that file. To find out the filename corresponding to an i-node we use the command *ncheck*. When given without an argument, *ncheck* gives a complete listing of the i-nodes of the file system. When used with the flag '-s' a listing of special files (i.e. those corresponding to I/O devices) and set-user-ID mode files (these can be set only by the superuser) is produced:

```
£ ncheck -s /dev/root
/dev/root:
92          /dev/console
91          /dev/mem
90          /dev/kmem
89          /dev/null
 .
 .
 .
```

When used with the flag '–i', *ncheck* gives the filenames corresponding to the i-numbers listed after the flag:

```
£ ncheck -i97 283 /dev/root
97          /dev/.
283         /etc/passwd
```

## Going into multi-user mode

Assuming that the checks on the system have been carried out successfully, the superuser may now put it into multi-user mode.

First, the system date should be set, by:

```
$ date [yymmddhhmm.ss]
```

with the obvious meanings. The seconds can be omitted if desired.

The system can now be put into multi-user mode. To do this, simply type ctrl-D. This causes file systems to be mounted and all terminals to run the *login* process. The system is now ready for multi-user access.

## 7.7 Mounting and Unmounting File systems

Devices such as floppies, tapes, etc. can be attached to the system for access to valid file systems on them and detached again by means of the *mount* and *umount* commands.

```
$ mount <device name> [-r]
```

and

```
$ umount <device name>
```

accomplish these operations.

The flag '*–r*', if present, means a read-only file system.


## 7.8 Bringing the System Down

The converse operation to startup is bringing the system down. The best rule to follow is that this should be avoided whenever possible, and this is so for a variety of reasons.

Firstly, it is best for most hardware to be kept running rather than to be subject to the power and temperature changes of being switched on and off. Second, the UNIX software is equipped with time-dependent procedures which will have to be restarted when the system is restarted. Some of these may have been frustrated by the switch-off, and they will have to be recommenced.

Third, bringing down the system may cause errors if it is done improperly. Processes may be halted while incomplete, and areas of disk may be incorrectly written. For these reasons halting the system should be avoided whenever possible. However, a switch-off is sometimes inevitable, for reasons of hardware or software maintenance or because UNIX itself crashes. Under such circumstances it is preferable that the system should be shutdown in good order.


### Shutdown command

The best way to bring the system down gracefully is to use the *shutdown* command. This specifies the length of time before the shutdown in minutes, and sends a message at one minute intervals to the system users telling them that shutdown is going to occur.

Users who logout will have their processes brought to an orderly conclusion; those who do not will eventually be logged out against their will. The *shutdown* command will halt all programs and processes, dismount all devices and halt the system:

```
$ shutdown
Minutes till shutdown? (0-15):    3
Broadcast message ...
UNIX shutdown in 3 minutes.
Clean up and log off.
.
.
.

All logged off now.
Broadcast message ...
UNIX will now terminate.
Kill -15 24 26
```

# 8 The Varieties of UNIX

## 8.1 Many Types of UNIX

UNIX exists in many different forms and incarnations. Some of these are dictated by different kinds of hardware, some by user convenience. In this chapter I shall outline the main varieties of UNIX and UNIX-like system in common circulation and explain which is appropriate for particular purposes. I shall start with a brief consideration of some of the factors which have determined the varieties of different types of UNIX which are in circulation at present.

### Portability

One of the biggest current software issues is that of portability – that is, how easy it is to take a piece of software from one hardware configuration to another. Ideally, one should be able to take a piece of software written for one machine and operating system and run it on any other machine and operating system. This is of course not possible.

Some sort of compromise can be reached however between different hardware environments under the same operating system, and so the goal of UNIX has been to provide variety and at the same time compatibility. The differences between the functionality of UNIX should be minimal across different implementations. Portability has long been one of the goals of UNIX, and one of the main points cited in its promotion.

Portability of the operating system implies ease of transposition of applications software from one machine to another. This is desirable either because there is more than one machine using the same software, or because one machine is replaced by another of more recent design, and you do not want to have extensive rewrites. The more portable the operating system, the lower should be the software costs involved.

UNIX is said to be easy to move from one piece of hardware to another, and therefore to be highly portable. To what extent is this true?

The elements of UNIX and their relation to the hardware are shown in Figure 1. There are three main parts to the UNIX kernel: the device drivers, the scheduler and the rest of the system including the file system and system calls.

The device drivers communicate with the hardware bus and through it to the input-output devices, such as hard and floppy disk and the console. The device drivers are the least portable part of UNIX and must be rewritten for new I/O buses and/or devices. The device drivers can however be written in C and, with a suitable C library, linked to the specific I/O bus concerned. This at least avoids having to write the whole of the driver routines in assembler.

The scheduler looks after the allocation of time and memory for processes. This entails communication with the processor and the memory mangament unit (MMU). The scheduler is thus partially machine-dependent but much of it can be written in portable C.

The rest of the kernel is concerned with the system calls (the primitives which the utilities depend upon) the file system and various extras. This part of UNIX can be written in C and should be completely portable.

## Porting UNIX

To carry out a port of UNIX to a new hardware environment, the required device drivers must be written or adapted from others to which (legitimate!) access is available. The scheduler must then be adapted if necessary to accommodate a new type of processor and MMU. Some of the basic utilities must then be transferred to the target machine, including the *mkfs* and *uucp* command programs which will enable a new file system to be created and the rest of the utilities downloaded. Various other modifications may need to be made in view of special hardware requirements, e.g. RAM disk drivers or special networking software.

The kernel then has to be constructed from these elements on the target machine and tested. This phase usually takes up the bulk of the time and effort, which may extend over only days (for the same processor in a different machine) or months for completely unfamiliar hardware.

It can be seen therefore that the claims to portability often made for

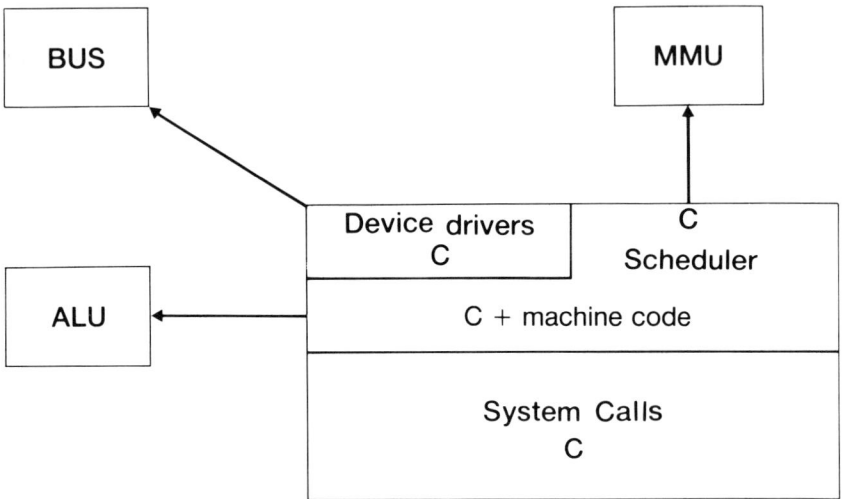

**Figure 1** Structure of UNIX

*Key*: ALU   Arithmetic and logic unit
       MMU  Memory management unit
       BUS   Data and address buses

UNIX can be misunderstood. There is no magic by which software can be moved from any type of machine to any other. UNIX makes the process easier, but problems are by no means eliminated.

## Reasons for the varieties of UNIX

### Hardware factors

UNIX originally evolved on a DEC PDP-7 (later on PDP-11s) and the system was therefore conceived of as most suitable for minicomputer systems. As has already been pointed out, UNIX has since migrated to many other kinds of computer system, from mainframes to micros and supermicros, and there have arisen types of UNIX which are well-adapted for these system types.

## Users' requirements

A further reason for differentiation between types of UNIX is differing user's requirements. UNIX was originally devised by systems programmers for systems programmers and its facilities were appropriate for such use. UNIX is now sold to the commercial market for end users and completely different kinds of facilities are demanded. This has also given rise to various types of 'user friendliness' such as menu-driven commands and WIMP interfaces, some of which have in turn been recycled for use by the systems programmer!

### Role of Bell Laboratories

A third factor in UNIX proliferation is the relationship which all UNIX systems have to the originators and intellectual property owners, Bell Laboratories. As everyone must surely know, even the name UNIX is a trademark of Bell Labs, and must not be used without attribution. The versions of UNIX themselves (unless they are complete rewrites as some are or claim to be) must pay dues to Bell for licensing. There are thus three distinct types of UNIX-like system. True UNIX from Bell or its subsidiaries, Bell-licensed systems produced by others, and non-Bell UNIX look-alikes or work-alikes.

Finally, there has been an attempt, the culmination of various efforts, to produce a UNIX standard, and this has resulted in Posix, the Institute of Electrical and Electronic Engineers (IEEE) standard UNIX. As with all standards its virtue is interchangeability, and its disadvantage is that the standard suits no-one as well as a tailor made job. The future of Posix looks bright but, obviously, is still to be assessed.

What we see today is thus a spectrum of UNIXes hopefully vying for the market which has been long-prophesied and long-awaited. To pick your way among them is no straightforward matter. The reader should bear in mind that things change very quickly in the world of computer software. The following information is for orientation purposes only, and one should look further before taking any decision.

## 8.2 Bell Labs UNIXes

### Early versions

The early versions of UNIX were known by version numbers using arabic numerals.

Version 1 was written for PDP-7 and PDP-9 minicomputers by Ken Thompson and Dennis Ritchie. Version 2 was for a PDP-11/20, the bottom of the PDP-11 range. Version 3 incorporated multi-programming and ran on most the then PDP-11s above and including the 11/34. This version embodied most of the main features of UNIX as it is now.

Version 4 ran only on the 11/70 and another 32-bit machine, the Interdata 8/32. Not much is known about Version 5.

The versions so far described were all internal to Bell Labs. Later internal editions have continued to be produced.

### Version 6

Version 6 was the first version external to Bell Labs. It was also the first UNIX to be sold for commercial use, though most of this use came from universities and research institutions rather than from commercial organisations.

Version 6 incorporated an improved file system and a wide range of commands and utilities.

### Version 7

This was the one widely sold during the early 1980s. It was also the one extensively licensed and imitated by others. The features of UNIX were mostly in place in this version, which was designed to be used and sold externally.

Version 7 had enhanced portability over Version 6, and an improved file system which, however, was not downwardly compatible with the V6 file system.

Later editions of UNIX were known by system numbers and roman numerals.

## System III

This version was designed for a fuller commercial exploitation than Version 7. While V7 had featurs which were mainly designed for the system programmer in academic or commercial fields, System III was also meant to be used by the applications programmer.

A project called the programmer's workbench (PWB) had been going on in Bell Labs since the late 1970s and some of these tools were incorporated into System III. The problems of remote job entry (RJE) arising on a large multiprogramming system and communications facilities in general were tackled and text processing was improved. Features were included such as the source code control system (SCCS) which enabled programmers to easily keep track of successive generations of files which were subject to modifications.

System III did not prove as popular as had been hoped and was rapidly succeeded by System V.

## System V

System V differs from System III in few basic respects, and mainly provdies enhanced speed and improvements to UNIX-to-UNIX communications (the *uucp* command), the addition of the screen editors *ex* and *vi* and one or two other improvements to libraries and commands. As a package System V was commercially acceptable, partly because it embodied the System V Interface Definition (SVID).

This was intended to be the 'standard' UNIX as far as Bell Labs were concerned. At the time of its announcement in 1982, Bell Labs pledged themselves to make no further radical alterations, e.g. to the file system standard, so that fufure compatibility would be assured. Upgrades from System III were offered at low cost.

In fact, successive modifications have been made disguised as release numbers. Thus, V.2 (System V, Release 2) incorporated features of Berkeley UNIX (see below), and Release 3 has features such as streams, remote file sharing (RFS), file system switch (FSS), the transport provider interface (TPI) which enhances the communication facilities of UNIX, and shared libraries.

## Release 3

The main features of Release 3 have been outlined above.

Streams was an innovation which allows communication between processes and character-oriented input-output devices. Like pipes, streams can be linearly connected in series, but unlike pipes they are two-way channels. Data can thus flow in both directions in a stream.

Remote file sharing is a feature enabling several UNIX systems running on different machines to communicate with each other through the same file system. Several of these types of facility have been proposed. In effect, the user can change to another machine as if it were part of his home machine's file system, subject of course to the necessary file permissions. RFS only links UNIX System V, Release 3 UNIXes together, however, while other file-sharing systems, e.g. the Newcastle Connection, are not so limited.

The file system switch allows several file systems in the same UNIX kernel. It does this by separating the UNIX system calls from the file system.

Shared libraries allows the linking of library routines at run time rather than at compile time, thus saving memory and disk space.

## 8.3 AT&T Licensed Versions

### XENIX

XENIX was a system originally written by Microsoft under license from AT&T, intended to be a commercially enhanced version of UNIX for such applications as this was appropriate. XENIX now also has a further aim – a degree of portability higher than that of standard UNIX. XENIX was originally written for PDP-11 minicomputers, but it is typically now associated with Intel-based micros, and is a commercially highly competitive version of UNIX. XENIX runs multi-user systems for varying numbers of users, although between two and ten users is most common, and it has been implemented for dozens of microcomputer systems.

XENIX was first developed by Microsoft, under license from AT&T and in conjunction with both Santa Cruz Operation (SCO) in the USA and Logica in the UK. XENIX was originally derived from UNIX V7 but has passed through a series of incarnations and now exists in a UNIX System V-compatible version, labelled variously as XENIX System V. The major microprocessor types, Intel, National Semiconductor and Motorola, have all been covered.

The recent position, arrived at through a series of deals, is that Microsoft and AT&T have announced a version of XENIX for Intel 80386 processor-based machines, which is compatible with UNIX V.3. Confusingly, this will be known under the name UNIX. This is the first time that the name UNIX will have been used for an AT&T licensed product.

The advantage of such a system will be that it provides a common standard for all 80286 and 80386 based systems. It will thus be applicable especially to the IBM PS/2 range of personal computers. It will have the further advantage that DOS systems for the PC and PS ranges will be implementable as processes under UNIX. The file formats for AT&T UNIX and for Intel processors will both be supported. UNIX for 80286 and 80386 will therefore be able to run UNIX and DOS side by side, offering considerable commercial advantages.

## Berkeley UNIX

While System V is the dominant version of UNIX in the commercial sector, the version most often found in the scientific and technical world is that developed at the University of California at Berkeley.

Berkeley UNIX is essentially a paging (virtual memory) version of UNIX for 32 bit computers, originally the DEC VAX computer range. The popularity of the VAX with the scientific community has ensured the development of a specialised UNIX along these lines. Berkeley UNIX has thus always been a 32 bit system, contrasted with the 16 bit origins of early AT&T versions.

The differences between Berkeley and AT&T UNIX go back some time. Before the commercial success of UNIX as a system, AT&T had licensed the development of UNIX for the DEC VAX range at Berkeley. There was in fact considerable collaboration between DEC and AT&T over this, although DEC itself has largely kept aloof from UNIX, seeing it as a rival to its own operating systems (see Ultrix, below).

Early Berkeley UNIX was known as 32V, and as the name implied was a 32 bit version of UNIX for virtual memory machines. A succession of licensable releases followed and were known under the name BSD (Berkeley Software Development). BSD is currently in release 4.3.

BSD includes facilities for command usage accounting, disk accounting and a range of tools for examining the status of the system while it is running, plus a tuning profiling tool. To this have been added good UNIX-to-UNIX communications.

BSD is preferred by academics, who are often equipped with VAXes, but is not reckoned to be of much commercial significance, except insofar as it has inspired other versions of UNIX to take up some of its tools.

## 8.4 UNIX-Like Systems

### Digital Equipment Corporation's Ultrix

The relationship of UNIX and DEC has always been an uneasy one. First written to run on 16-bit DEC machines, and later adapted for 32-bit equipment, UNIX would seem to be an ideal medium for expanding DEC's popularity. DEC themselves have not seen it in this light. Their attitude towards their products has always been highly proprietorial. Their philosophy asserts that as far as possible their software should run only on their hardware, and their hardware should run only their own software. UNIX as an alien operation system was seen as a direct rival to DEC PDP 11 and VAX operating systems.

However, one must be a realist, and such is the popularity of UNIX as an operating system for DEC hardware that DEC themselves were compelled to provide versions of UNIX of their own. That for the PDP-11 was known as V7M-11. The version for VAX is called Ultrix. They also have a version for the Professional micro called Venix. Venix is of little interest except to Professional users, who are relatively sparse anyway, and most PDP-11s run a version of UNIX, so that the only important UNIX-like DEC product is Ultrix.

Ultrix Version 2 offers most of the functions necessary to conform to the SVID standard. However it still differs from SVID, mainly in terms of terminal attributes. DEC have therefore apparently turned back from their original intention of producing a fully SVID-compatible version of Ultrix.

DEC have lately supported the IEEE standard known initially as P1003, and latterly Posix. Their reason for this is probably that Posix virtually conforms to SVID which gives it credibility, but is not actually System V. DEC is thus got out of the awkward situation of being seen to support rival software, while still conforming to an internationally acceptable standard.

## Whitesmith's Idris

Whitesmith's Idris is perhaps the most complete attempt to set up an alternative UNIX-like operating system. In addition to having the advantages of UNIX structure, Idris is claimed to offer a more complete degree of portability than UNIX itself. The philosophy of Idris is to try to make as much of the kernel as possible independent of hardware. The device drivers and memory management are of course the two exceptions.

The portability of Idris depends on its associated C compiler. Once this has been ported to a target system the rest of Idris can be transferred to that system fairly readily. It is claimed that more than 90 per cent of Idris is machine-independent.

The main drawback with Idris is that it has been modelled around obsolescent versions of UNIX and does not offer the variety of system calls and facilities which can now be got in UNIX. Nevertheless complete system-call compatibility with some versions of UNIX is claimed.

## Minix

AT&T was initially very keen to have UNIX used in academic institutions. The licence fee for UNIX was accordingly set very much lower to Universities compared to the charge to commercial users. This policy was presumably dictated by the notion that students coming out ready trained in UNIX and seeing its advantages would spread the good news and demand UNIX in their working environment.

However, this policy later changed. At the time of Version 7, AT&T decided to limit the use of source code and decreed that it should not be used for teaching purposes. Lecturers were thus left without a model to use as a basis for the discusssion of structured operating systems of the UNIX type.

This gap has now been filled by a version of UNIX called Minix. Minix is the work of Andrew Tannenbaum and his students at the Free University of Amsterdam. Minix is system-call compatible with Version 7 UNIX, but is completely rewritten and is said not to contain a single line of UNIX source code. This claim, unlike those of some commercial UNIX lookalikes, seems completely credible.

Minix does not offer the whole range of utilities of V7, but it does cover the basic ones, such as *cat, chmod, cmpdate* and so on. It has a C compiler which is also a completely original piece of work.

The Minix shell is compatible with the Bourne shell of V7 and the system calls of V7 are implemented with a few exceptions. The source code is of course obtainable for teaching purposes.

## Mark Williams Coherent

Claiming to be a complete rewrite of UNIX in original code, it apparently follows UNIX to a fault.

## Unice

Australian-style UNIX from Wollongong University.

## Unos

Charles Rivers' Data Systems version.

## Xelos

Perkin Elmer Data Systems version.

# Index

"(append to file) 84
£ define 84
\ (escape character) 81, 102, 105
? (file expansion character) 60
.profile 72
< (redirect from) 59, 60
> (redirect to) 59, 60
/ (root directory) 50
/bin 51
/dev 52
/etc 54
/lib 55
/user 19, 55
/usr 55
/usr/bin 56
/usr/lib 56

ac (accounting) 22–23
appending to file 59, 62
arrays 87
ASCII 36
automatic variable 93
awk (pattern processing) 118

Bell Labs and UNIX 141–143
block structure 77, 88
bootstrap 1, 2
Bourne shell 74
braces { } 81
bringing down UNIX 136

C compiler 76–77, 80, 180
C language 76–95
cc (C compile) 80
case (C) 89
case (shell) 69
cd (change directory) 18
char 86
chmod (change mode) 9, 66
chown (change ownership) 131
clri (clear i-node) 134
cmp (compare files) 20–21, 49

Coherent 148
comm (compare files) 21, 49
commenting 82
cp (copy file) 18
creating files 12–13

dcheck (directory check) 134
declaration 78
deleting files 38
deroff (strip roff constructs) 23–24
device name 42, 52–53
device handling 5, 42
diff (find differences) 21
diff 3 (three way differences) 24–25
directories 15–17, 40–42, 50–57
  parent and child 20, 42
do...while 77
do...done 65
double 87

ed (text editor) 12–14, 46–47, 96–108
  // (search) 104
  a (append) 96, 97
  character sets 106
  d (delete) 97
  g (global search) 103
  i (insert) 97
  j (join) 100
  matching characters 104–107
  p (print) 97
  q (quit editor) 14
  s (substitute) 98
  u (undo) 100
environment 72
escape sequence 80
executable file 59, 74
export (exporting parameters) 73
extern 92

file (find file type) 25
file handling 2–3, 46

file-oriented device 5
file security 44
file system 36–57
    map 50–57
file type
    directory 40–41
    ordinary 37–40, 41
    special 42–43
filter 64
flags 17
*float* 85, 87
flow control (C) 83, 88–89
flow control (shell) 67–69
*for* (C) 77
*for* (shell) 68
fork 60–62
functions (C) 90

*grep* (find patterns) 68
goto 77, 86

here document 72
HOME 72
home directory 11, 41

i-list 38
i-node 38
i-number 38–39
*icheck* (file system check) 135
Idris 147
if...elif 68
if...else 77, 88
initialising 83
input-output 85
*int* 85, 86

job scheduling 2, 6
*join* (relational database) 25, 49

*lex* (lexical analyser) 120–122
link 26, 41
link count 38
listing files 13, 15, 47
*ln* (make link to file) 26–27, 49
*look* (find lines in file) 27
loops 67, 82

MAIL 72
*mail* (electronic mail) 29
*man* (on-line UNIX manual) 27–28
*mkdir* (make directory) 9, 16
*mount* (attach file system) 39, 136
moving files 28, 48
*mv* (change filename) 28, 48

*ncheck* (list i-nodes) 135
newline character 37
*nice* (run at low priority) 29
*nm* (symbol table) 29–30
*nroff* (typewriter roff) 116

*od* (octal dump) 30–31
others group 45
others in own group 45
own group 45
ownership 131

*passwd* (set password) 31–32
PATH 72
pathnames 20, 41
permission bits 53, 56
permit directory 45
pipe 33, 43, 60–61
pipeline 62
pointers 94
portability 138–139
*pr* (print file) 16, 48
*prep* (separate words of file) 64
priority 29
programming style 83
*pwd* (print current directory) 19

quitting editor 14

*read* (assign variable value) 73
*readonly* (protect variable) 73
redirection 43–44, 60, 62
regular expression 47, 117
*rm* (remove file) 32
*rmdir* (remove directory) 32
*roff* (text formatting) 113–116
root 40, 50

scope 91–92
screen editor
    adding text 109–110
    moves 110–111

150

quitting 109
  searching 112
  terminal type 108
search path 59
*sed* (stream editor) 119–120
*sh* (invoke shell) 66
shell 9, 58–60
shell programs (scripts) 64–69
shift 70
*sort* (sort a file) 49
standard input/output 63
starting up UNIX 132–136
string variables 71
structures 93
static variable 93
*stty* (set up terminal) 32
substitutable parameters 69–70
super-block 38
superuser 40, 45, 125–137
switch 89
system calls 59
system checks 133–136


*tail* (get tail of file) 33
*tee* (t-joint in a pipe) 33
TERM 72
*test* (find file status) 71
text buffer 46
*time* (get time and date) 33. 46
*touch* (update last access) 33–34

*tr* (transliterate) 34
*tty* (find terminal number) 34
*troff* (typesetting roff) 116
typing 77–78

Ultrix 146
*umount* (detach file system) 39, 136
Unice 148
union 78
*uniq* (find duplicate lines) 34, 49
UNIX
  lookalikes 55, 146–148
  resident 51
  structure 139–140
  style 8
until...do 67

Unos 148
user-friendliness 8
user group 40, 45
users
  adding 128–130
  removing 131–132

*vi* (screen editor) 14, 108

*while* 83

Xelos 148

*yacc* (input structuring) 122–124